BONDS

Loyalty, Lies, and the Life That Almost Killed Me

BY ROGER BONDS

DISCLAIMER

The advice contained in this material might not be suitable for everyone. The authors designed the information to present their opinion about the subject matter. The reader must carefully investigate all aspects of any business decision before committing to him or herself. The authors obtained the information contained herein from sources they believe to be reliable and from their own personal experiences, but they neither imply nor intend any guarantee of accuracy. The authors are not in the business of giving legal, accounting, or any other type of professional advice. Should the reader need such advice, he or she must seek services from a competent professional. The authors particularly disclaims any liability, loss, or risk taken by individuals who directly or indirectly act on the information contained herein. The authors believe the advice presented here is sound, but readers cannot hold them responsible for either the actions they take, or the risk taken by individuals who directly or indirectly act on the information contained herein.

Published by 1Brick Publishing
Printed in the United States
Copyright © 2026 by Roderick Rowan
ISBN 979-8898560270

DEDICATION

To the young men and women who learned loyalty before they learned choice, the survivors who were told silence was strength, and everyone standing at a crossroads, trying to decide
 whether to stay bound to what they know or risk becoming who they were meant to be.

This book is for you.

EPIGRAPH

"Word is Bond: Built on No Deception"

They say loyalty is everything.
But loyalty to the wrong things will kill you.
Loyalty to silence.
Loyalty to people who don't deserve it.
Loyalty to a version of yourself that was never free.

This is what I know now:
Real loyalty starts with the truth.
And the truth will cost you everything you thought you needed.

This is my bond.
This is my word.

— Roger "Bonds" Rowan

AUTHOR'S NOTE

I didn't write this book to be famous. I wrote it because I spent most of my life protecting the wrong things. Protecting people who didn't protect me. Protecting codes that never protected anybody. Protecting silence when silence was killing me from the inside out.

For years, people asked me, "Bonds, when you gonna tell your story?" And I'd say, "One day."

But the truth is, I wasn't ready. Because telling this story means admitting things I'm not proud of. It means looking at the kid I was, the man I became, and the choices I made that I can't take back. It means talking about things that powerful people would rather I keep quiet about.

But in 2024, I got diagnosed with prostate cancer. And when you're sitting in a doctor's office at 58 years old, listening to them tell you that your body is breaking down because of the stress you carried, the secrets you kept, the life you lived—you realize something.

Silence will kill you faster than a bullet ever will. So this book is my truth. All of it. The good, the bad, the ugly, and the parts that still keep me up at night.

WHO THIS BOOK IS FOR

If you're reading this and you're young—still trying to figure out who you are, what loyalty means, whether the block is all you got—this is for you.

If you're reading this from a cell—doing time, thinking about what's next, wondering if anybody out here gives a damn—this is for you.

If you're reading this and you've been hurt by someone you trusted, someone you worked for, someone you loved—this is for you.

If you're reading this and you're trapped in something that looks good on the outside but feels like hell on the inside—this is for you.

And if you're reading this because you saw my name in the headlines, in a lawsuit, in a documentary, and you want to know what really happened—I'm going to tell you. But not the way you think.

WHAT THIS BOOK IS ABOUT

This is a book about loyalty. But not the kind of loyalty they sell you in the streets or in the industry. This is about what happens when loyalty becomes a cage. When it stops being about brotherhood and starts being about survival. When you're so deep in it that you can't tell the difference between protecting someone and protecting yourself.

This is a book about silence. The kind of silence that feels like strength but is really fear. The kind of silence that makes you complicit in things you know are wrong. The kind of silence that eats you alive.

This is a book about power. Real power versus access. The difference between being close to money and actually having it. The difference between being in the room and actually having a voice.

And this is a book about breaking free. Not in some Hollywood way where everything ends perfect. But in the real way. The hard way. The way where you lose things. Where people turn on you. Where you have to rebuild yourself from scratch.

WHAT I'M NOT GOING TO DO

I'm not going to lie to make myself look better. I'm not going to pretend I was just an innocent bystander. I'm not going to glorify the violence, the drugs, the street life, or the industry life. And I'm not going to tell you I have all the answers, because I don't. But I'm going to tell you what I learned. And I'm going to tell you what it cost me.

A WORD ABOUT THE PEOPLE IN THIS BOOK

Some of the people in this story are dead. Some are in prison. Some are free and trying to forget who they used to be.

I've changed some names to protect people who deserve protection. But the people who did harm? I'm calling it what it is. Not because I'm bitter. Not because I want revenge. But because silence protects predators, and I'm done being silent.

If you're reading this and you were there—you know what happened. You know what you saw. You know what you did or didn't do.

That's between you and your conscience.

This is between me and mine.

WHY NOW

People ask me, "Why speak up now? Why not ten years ago? Why not twenty?" And the truth is: I wasn't ready.I was still too close to it. Still too loyal. Still too afraid of what I'd lose. But when my son got locked up, when my marriage fell apart, when I got cancer, when I watched people I knew get destroyed by the same system I was part of—I realized something.

The cost of staying silent was higher than the cost of telling the truth.

And the people who need to hear this story—the young cats in the hood, the men in cells, the women trapped in abusive situations, the people working for powerful predators and convincing themselves it's normal— they need to hear it now.

Not when it's convenient. Not when it's safe. Now.

WHAT I HOPE YOU GET FROM THIS

I hope you see yourself in these pages. Not because you lived my exact life, but because you've felt what I felt. The pressure. The fear. The loyalty that became a trap. The moment when you knew something was wrong but you stayed anyway.

I hope this book makes you think about your own bonds. Who you're loyal to. What you're protecting. What it's costing you.

And I hope—more than anything—that this book gives you permission to choose differently.

You are not your zip code. You are not your past. You are not who they say you have to be. You are your next decision.

This is my story. This is my testimony. This is my bond.

Word is Bond: Built On No Deception.

Let's go.

— **Roger Bonds**
Atlanta, GA, 2026

TABLE OF CONTENTS

PROLOGUE

THE NIGHT EVERYTHING CHANGED

Madison Square Garden, New York City
October 2004

The music stops. Twenty thousand people at Madison Square Garden, packed in for the "Best of Both Worlds" tour—Jay-Z and R. Kelly, two of the biggest names in music on one stage—and suddenly, R. Kelly stops performing. Just stops. Mid-song. It's me, Puff, and my man Black. Paul, who is head of security, didn't feel like coming in tonight. He told us, "You and Puff, just go in." So we're at Madison Square Garden. At what was supposed to be the biggest tour of the year. And something is about to go very wrong.

Kelly's talking to the crowd, telling them he sees something. Guns. He's saying he sees guns in the crowd. MSG security sweeps the arena. They find nothing. No guns. No threats. Nothing. But the tension is thick. This tour has been a disaster from day one. Missed rehearsals. Arguments. Kelly showing up late or not showing up at all. Jay trying to keep it professional while Kelly's acting like he's doing everybody a favor just by being there. This has been building for weeks. And now it's about to explode.

Kelly decides he's going back on stage. I can see his crew moving, getting ready to go back out there. And that's when all the lights go out. Complete darkness. Twenty thousand people. Total silence for three seconds. And I know—this is it. This is when it happens. When the lights come back on, Puff turns to me. "Yo, is that real?" "I don't know," I say. "I'm out here just like you." He takes off running toward the backstage. I'm right behind him.

We get backstage and it's chaos. Jay-Z is standing there, and I can see it in his face—he doesn't know what to do. Puff walks right up to Jay. "Yo, listen," he says. "Get it together." And then he does something I'll never forget. He takes the chain off his own neck and puts it on Jay. "All of us is out here," Puff tells him. "Me, Mary (Mary J. Blige), Ja (Ja Rule) everybody. We got you." It's a moment. A real moment. Puff trying to calm the situation, trying to give Jay some strength, some solidarity.

Jay gets on stage and starts performing, the crowd is going crazy, he's performing "Empire State of Mind." A few moments later, Kelly and his crew are pushing to get back on stage, and little does Jay know the whole situation is about to go in a direction no one expected. As Kelly's entourage are trying to get on stage, Ty Ty pulls out the mace. And he sprays. Kelly's two bodyguards get hit. People are rushing in. Yelling. Kelly's crew is trying to get at Ty Ty. And I see guns. Real guns. People pulling out hardware, and I know—if this goes any further, somebody's getting killed tonight.

I move. I swing on one of Kelly's people—not to hurt them, just to create space, to break the momentum. I grab Puff and throw him behind me.

Puff looks at me and tell me to get "Ty Ty up outta here and take him to Daddy's House." The police are coming. The building's about to lock down. And Ty Ty just pepper-sprayed three people in front of everyone backstage. "Run!" I yell at Ty. We take off across the stage—me and Ty Ty, running through the backstage area, through the corridors, people yelling behind us.

We hit the exit, but when we get outside, Ty Ty flags down a yellow cab, jumps in and tells me "Bonds, I'm good! Good Looking out!" MSG is on lockdown. The police are looking for him. The concert is still going. But Ty Ty's safe.

Later that day, Jay-Z calls Puff. "Yo," Jay says. "Ty told me one of your homeboys helped him. Who was that?" "That's my man Bonds," Puff says. "He just came home." A few hours later, Puff calls me. "Yo, Jay wants to meet you. Meet me at 40/40." We pull up to 40/40 Club—Jay's spot in Manhattan. Jay shakes my hand. "Ty told me what you did," he says. "You got him out of there." I nod. "That's what I do. Plus he got a lot of heart." He looks at me and says "he's always been like that." We dap again then Jay says. "Well, if you ever need anything, you let me know."

That same night, Puff takes me to Mr. Chow's to eat. It's me, him, and a few of his people. And he's telling them the story. "Yo, you should've seen how this nigga moved," he says. "These niggas had joints out, it was crazy, and Bonds grabbed me, threw me behind him like a shield then I told him to get Ty Ty, so he got him out of there." Puff looks at Paul, his current Head of Security and says "I'm cool with Bonds just being with me." I guess this was where I proved myself and showed how I would handle things under pressure. That was the first day I was actually holding Puff down. And that's how it all started.

I was 32 years old. I'd just come home from doing five years in federal prison. Before that, I did time for a body I caught when I was 19. I'd spent my whole life in the streets—Harlem, Polo Grounds, Baltimore, hustling, surviving, doing whatever I had to do to stay alive. And now I'm being handed a golden ticket. A chance to travel the world. Private jets. Access to power. A front-row seat to the life I'd only seen on TV. Why wouldn't I take it?

But here's what I didn't know. I didn't know that the loyalty I showed that night—the same loyalty that got me the job—would become the cage that almost destroyed me. I didn't know that protecting Puff would mean protecting things I couldn't live with. I didn't know that being in the room would mean staying silent about what happened in the room. I didn't know that proximity to power is not the same thing as having power. And I didn't know that twenty years later, I'd be sitting in a doctor's office with a cancer diagnosis, looking back at my life and asking myself: Was it worth it?

The R. Kelly and Jay-Z situation was a warning. A warning about what happens when egos clash, when respect breaks down, when people with power decide the rules don't apply to them. Kelly got banned from MSG. Kicked off the tour. Filed a $75 million lawsuit. Jay-Z fired back publicly, and the "Best of Both Worlds" tour—the thing that was supposed to be the biggest collaboration in hip-hop and R&B—was over. Just like that.

But that night also taught me something else. It taught me that loyalty is currency in this world. That if you prove you'll move when things get dangerous, you become valuable. That if you show you'll protect people when everybody else is running, you earn your place. I learned that lesson well. Too well.

This is the story of what happened next. The parties. The jets. The money. The manipulation. The abuse I witnessed. The silence I kept. The moment I realized I was part of something I couldn't defend. And the choice I had to make when the world finally started asking questions I'd been avoiding for years. This is the story of how I became Bonds. And how I almost lost myself trying to be loyal to someone who was never loyal to me.

They say word is bond. But what happens when your bond is built on lies? What happens when your loyalty is to someone who sees you as disposable? What happens when the life you thought you wanted becomes the life that's killing you? I'm about to tell you. Every bit of it. The good, the bad, and the ugly. Because silence protects the powerful. And I'm done being silent. Let's go.

ACT I:
THE CODE

PART ONE:
POLO GROUNDS

CHAPTER 1

BORN IN THE FIRE

Harlem, New York
1970s

I was born at Sydenham Hospital on 125th Street in 1967. My mother brought me home to the Johnson Projects on the East Side. A Dope Fiends Heaven where it's literally the Night of the Living Dead. At the same time, it's the kind of place where you knew everybody, and everybody knew your business. We lived there until I was about seven years old. Then we moved to Polo Grounds. And that's where everything changed.

Polo Grounds was different. It wasn't just projects. It was a world. A whole ecosystem with its own rules, its own hierarchy, its own code. You had people there who were getting money—real money—but they just didn't want to leave. They felt comfortable. Safe. They had family there, history there. Their kids went to school with other kids from the projects, and on the weekends, they'd pull up in the latest cars, park in the lot, and act like it was the most normal thing in the world. I'm talking about Black families with money. Legal money. Fathers who worked good jobs. Mothers who dressed sharp. Kids who wore sheepskin coats and had the newest sneakers. You'd walk to school with cats whose parents had Cadillacs and Lincolns parked downstairs.

That was one side of Polo Grounds. The other side? Hustlers. Stick-up kids. Dudes who were getting money in the streets or taking it from somebody else. And the crazy thing is, they lived in the same buildings. Sometimes on the same floor. You had Building One beefing with Building Two. Building Two beefing with Building Three. But if somebody from outside the projects tried us? All four buildings came together. That was the code. Protect the projects. Protect your people. Even if you didn't like them, even if you had beef with them inside the walls—outside those walls, we were one.

My father was there. But he wasn't there. You know what I mean? He'd be there in the morning when you woke up. No matter what happened the night before, no matter what he did, where he went, who he was with—he'd be there in the morning. Sitting at the table. Making sure we had something to eat. Acting like everything was normal. But at night? He was gone. And when he was there, it was hell.

See, my father had four other kids with other women. But me, my two older sisters, my older brother, and my younger brother—we were all from the same mother and the same father. All five of us in the same house. And we all heard it. The fighting. The yelling. And the Disrespect! I was young, but I wasn't too young to understand what was happening. You can't unhear certain sounds. You can't unsee certain things.

My father was abusive. Not to us. To her. He would belittle her and talk to her in ways that could mentally destroy even the strongest person. And we'd sit there, listening, not knowing what to do. Not knowing if we should run in there or stay in our rooms. Not knowing if getting involved would make it worse. I remember nights when I'd put my pillow over my head, trying to block it out. I remember mornings when my mother would come out with her head up high, acting as if nothing ever happened. And my father would sit there at the breakfast table like he was Father of the Year.

That's what I grew up watching. That's what I thought a man was supposed to be. Strong. In control. Unbreakable. Even if it meant breaking everybody else.

My mother finally left him. I don't remember exactly when, but I remember the day she told me she was taking my younger brother with her and I had to stay with my father. I was maybe thirteen, fourteen. "Why I gotta stay?" I asked her. She didn't really have an answer. Or maybe she did, and I just didn't want to hear it. All I know is, she left. My little brother went with her. And I was stuck in that apartment with a man who was hardly ever there.

And that's when I got my first taste of freedom. Not the good kind. The dangerous kind. The kind where there's no curfew. No rules. No consequences. The kind where a kid can become whoever he wants to be. And I wanted to be like the dudes I saw outside.

Polo Grounds had everything. You wanted to see what success looked like? There were people there who had it. Clean jobs. Nice clothes. Respect. You wanted to see what the street life looked like? There were dudes there who had that too. Money. Power. Fear. The question was: which side were you going to choose? And for most of us, it wasn't really a choice. It was whatever grabbed your attention first.

For me, it was the flash. The cars. The jewelry. The way dudes moved with confidence, like they owned the block. I'd see them on 155th Street, on Eighth Avenue, posted up in front of the buildings, money in their pockets, girls around them, respect in their eyes. And I'd think: That's what I want. I didn't think about the consequences. I didn't think about the bodies that came with that life. I didn't think about the jail cells or the funerals. I just saw what I wanted to see. And I started moving toward it.

People always ask me: "Bonds, why didn't you go the other way? You had examples of people doing it right. Why didn't you follow them?" And the truth is, I don't have a good answer. I could blame my father. I could blame the environment. I could blame the lack of guidance or the absence of a strong male figure who wasn't violent. But the truth is, I made a choice. I chose the flashy life. I chose the streets. And once you make that choice, it's hard as hell to turn back.

By the time I was thirteen, I was already running with older dudes. I wasn't deep in the game yet. I was just around it. Watching. Learning. I'd run errands for cats. Go to the store for them. Hold something for them if they needed me to. They'd give me twenty dollars, and I'd feel like a king. Twenty dollars at thirteen years old? That was everything. That was a new pair of sneakers. That was being able to buy my own food. That was not having to ask my mother for anything. And more than that, it was respect.

When you're a kid in the projects and older dudes know your name, that means something. It means you're not invisible. It means you matter. And I wanted to matter.

I remember the first time I went into the game room on Eighth Avenue. I was about thirteen. This dude named Boo came up to me and said, "Yo, little Bonds, you want to work in the game room?" Hell yeah, I wanted to work in the game room. The game room was where everybody went. It was where you played video games, ate chips, drank soda, and acted like you were somebody. If you worked there, you were cool by default.

So I started working there. Fifty dollars a day. Cash. I didn't realize at the time who really owned the place. I didn't know that Preacher and Small Paul were the ones behind it. I didn't know that when the cops ran up in there looking for guns, it was because those dudes were so hot that the police couldn't leave them alone. I was just happy to be getting paid. I was happy to have the girls coming in, seeing me behind the counter, thinking I was that dude. I was happy to be part of something. Even if I didn't fully understand what that something was.

Looking back now, I see it clearly. Polo Grounds gave me options. I could've gone to school every day. I could've focused on my grades. I could've followed the example of the kids whose parents had good jobs and clean money. But I didn't. I followed the flash. I followed the dudes who had money in their pockets and guns on their waists. I followed the excitement.

And once you start down that road, it's hard to stop. Because the streets don't just take your time. They take your mind. They make you believe that this is all there is. That this is all you'll ever be. They make you believe that the only way to be somebody is to be feared. And by the time you realize it's a lie, you're already too deep to turn back.

I was born in the fire. Sydenham Hospital. Johnson Projects. Polo Grounds. Domestic violence. Absent fathers. Streets that raised me when nobody else would. That fire shaped me. It made me tough. It made me loyal. It made me willing to do whatever it took to survive. But it also made me blind. Blind to the fact that the life I was chasing was the same life that destroyed everybody who came before me. Blind to the fact that loyalty to the wrong things would cost me everything. Blind to the fact that I had a choice. I just didn't know it yet.

CHAPTER 2

THE FLASHY LIFE

Harlem, 1980-1982
Ages 13-15

Before I ever touched real drugs, I was already living like a hustler. I just didn't know it yet. It started with the paper routes.

Every Sunday morning, me and my boys would wake up early—I'm talking 5 a.m.—and we'd run the Sunday papers through the projects. You'd get your stack of newspapers, and you'd hit every floor, every apartment, screaming through the hallways: "NEWSPAPER! SUNDAY PAPER!" Sounds simple, right? It wasn't. Because in the projects, the paper route was just like the drug game.

You had your building. That was your territory. If another kid came through your building screaming "NEWSPAPER," you had a problem. That was your customers. Your money. Your block. I'm serious. We'd be out there protecting our paper routes like we were protecting a corner. "Yo, this is my building. You can't come through here." And if somebody tried? We'd fight over it. Over newspapers. But it made sense to us.

Because even at thirteen, we understood territory. We understood money. We understood that if you let somebody take what's yours, you're weak.

Me and my boy would split the money 50/50. On a good Sunday, we'd make about $100 each. A hundred dollars at thirteen years old. That was everything. That was new sneakers. That was going to the store and buying whatever you wanted. That was not having to ask your mother for lunch money. But more than that, it was the feeling. The feeling of having your own money. The feeling of not depending on nobody. The feeling of being able to move like the older dudes. Because we'd take that money and go straight to AJ Lester.

If you know, you know. AJ Lester was the store. THE store. It was on 125th Street, and if you didn't have something from AJ Lester, you weren't fly. We're talking British Walkers. Leather jackets. The kind of clothes that made people turn their heads when you walked down the street. Even if all you could afford was a T-shirt from AJ Lester, you'd walk out of there with that bag, holding it up so everybody could see it. Because the bag was just as important as what was inside. It said: I got money. I'm somebody. And at thirteen, that's all I wanted to be. Somebody.

Every morning during the school year, we had a routine. We'd meet in front of the projects at eight o'clock sharp, and we'd catch an OJ car service—straight to school. Number 66. I'll never forget that number. Every single morning, Number 66 would pull up, and we'd pile in. Five, six deep. All of us dressed fly. British Walkers. Sheepskin coats if you had it. Fresh haircuts. We'd pull up to Wagner Junior High School like we owned the place. Girls would be outside, watching us get out of that car, and we felt like kings. It didn't matter that we lived in the projects. It didn't matter that half of us were failing classes. What mattered was how we looked. How we moved. How people saw us.

That's where the peer pressure started. Not from adults. Not from teachers or parents. From each other. If you pulled up one day without the right sneakers, without the right jacket, without the right look—people noticed. "Yo, what happened? You broke now?" "Yo, where you get them sneakers from? Nobody wearing those no more." It sounds stupid now, but back then? That pressure was real. Because if you couldn't keep up, you fell behind. And if you fell behind, you became invisible. So you did whatever you had to do to stay fresh. You ran those paper routes. You hustled. You asked your moms for money even though you knew she didn't have it. Or, if you were like me, you started looking for other ways to get it.

They called me "Con Ed." Before anybody was getting called "Lights Out," that was my name in Polo Grounds. Con Ed. Because I'd put your lights out. You could go up there right now and ask anybody who knew me back then. They'd tell you. But it wasn't just about being able to fight. It was about how we handled beefs.

See, in Polo Grounds, we had a system. A ritual. The buildings went up to the 30th floor. And we had keys to the elevators—stolen from the maintenance men. If you were really somebody in your building, you had a key to the elevator. That was mandatory. When you had beef with somebody from your building, you didn't jump them. You didn't shoot them. You didn't let it drag out. You handled it in the elevator.

Here's how it worked: You and whoever you had beef with would get in the elevator. Just the two of you. Nobody else allowed. Then one of us would put the key in and lock it so it wouldn't stop on any floor. First floor to the 30th floor. Then back down from the 30th to the first. And you fought. The elevator was so tiny you'd be bumping into each other, into the walls. Boom, boom, boom, boom. No escape. No running. No getting jumped because nobody else could get in. Just you and him until one of you won or you both got tired.

And when that elevator came back down to the first floor? The beef was squashed. Done. Over. You might see each other in the lobby the next day and nod. Your mothers would still talk. Your families would still be cool. Because you handled it like men. One on one. Fair fight.

That system saved lives. Saved a lot of beefs from carrying on. Saved a lot of people from getting shot over stupid shit. Because at the end of the day, your mother was talking to his mother. Your father—if you had one— was talking to his father. Y'all lived in the same building. So you fought it out and moved on. That's why they called me Con Ed. Because when it was time to get in that elevator, I was putting your lights out.

Building Four—we called it Vietnam because it was just crazy over there—that's where my homeboy Boo was from. Boo was bananas with his hands too. We'd go round after round in that elevator sometimes just to see who was better. That's how you earned respect in Polo Grounds. Not by shooting. Not by jumping people. By being able to handle your-self one-on-one. And I could handle myself.

By the time I was fifteen, I was working in the game room. This cat named Boo came up to me one day and said, "Yo, little Bonds, we open-ing up a game room on Eighth Avenue. You want to be in there?" Hell yeah, I wanted to be in there. The game room was the spot. That's where everybody came to play Pac-Man, Donkey Kong, Galaga—all the games we couldn't afford to have at home. And if you worked there? You were automatically cool. You had access. You could let people play for free if you wanted. You could hook your boys up with sodas and chips. Girls came through all the time. It was the perfect setup.

So I took the job. Fifty dollars a day. Cash. I thought I was getting money. But here's the thing I didn't know. I didn't know who I was really working for. See, two dudes would come through every day. They'd check on the spot, make sure everything was running smooth, make sure I had enough quarters, enough supplies. "Yo, Bonds, you good? You need anything?" "Nah, I'm good." "Aight, cool. Keep it up." They were always polite. Always respectful. But I didn't realize that those two dudes—those two dudes who treated me like I mattered—were Preacher and Small Paul.

If you don't know those names, let me tell you: these were serious people. Preacher was one of the most respected—and feared—dudes in Harlem. Him and Small Paul ran things. Real things. And the game room? That wasn't just a game room. It was a front. I didn't figure it out until later, but the police were always running up in there. "Where the guns at? Where the drugs at?" And I'd be standing there like, "What are you talking about? This is a game room." But they weren't looking for me. They were looking for Preacher. For Small Paul. For whoever else was using that spot to move work or stash weapons.

I was just the kid behind the counter, completely clueless, thinking I had a regular job. But the respect I was getting? That wasn't because I was running a game room. It was because I was working for them. And in Harlem, if Preacher and Small Paul knew your name, that meant something.

There was this dude in the projects named Mike. Another OG. Another name that carried weight. Mike was getting money, but he was also the kind of dude who people didn't play with. He was smooth. Quiet. But Dangerous. And I was around all of them. Not because I was in the streets yet. Not because I was doing anything illegal. But because I was young, I was available, and I was willing to work.

They'd give me twenty dollars just to run to the store and get some orange juice or some chips. Twenty dollars for a five-minute errand. And I'd do it, thinking I was just helping out. But what I was really doing was learning. Learning how they moved. Learning how they talked. Learning how they handled business. Learning what loyalty looked like. What respect looked like. What power looked like. And I wanted that.

Here's what I didn't understand at the time. These dudes were teaching me the game without teaching me the consequences. They were showing me the money, the respect, the flash—but they weren't showing me the bodies, the prison cells, the funerals. I didn't see Preacher go to jail. I didn't see Small Paul lose people close to him. I didn't see the cost. All I saw was the reward. And when you're fifteen years old, living in the projects, with a father who's barely there and a mother who's struggling—that reward looks like everything.

I remember one time with a dude named G-Man. G-Man was one of those guys who lived in and out of jail. Never worked out, but was just built like that. Strong for no reason. He was about six or seven years older than me, and he had a reputation. A bully type. The kind who tested people just to see who they were. As I started getting older and making a little money in the streets, G-Man noticed. And once he noticed, the little tests started. Small things. Little moments. Just enough to see if I had heart. Just enough to see if I'd fold.

One day I was getting into the elevator, and G-Man jumped in behind me. We rode all the way up to the 19th floor. As soon as the doors opened, he tapped my pockets. And growing up, one thing you learn early is this: don't ever let nobody tap your pockets. Now mind you, G-Man was way bigger than me at the time. He had just come home from jail. Muscles sitting on top of his shoulders. That jail strength. I was nervous, but I knew something in that moment. If I folded once, this wouldn't be the last time.

He looked at me and said, "You got twenty dollars?" I did have money. I had about $120 in my pocket. But I looked him dead in his face and said, "Nah." He stared at me for a second. Then he let it go.

About a week later, I ran into him again. This time, I was carrying two boxes of brand-new all-white sneakers. There was no hiding nothing then. He reached for the bag and tried to snatch it from me. And something in me clicked. I pulled out my knife. Not because I wanted to use it. Not because I was tough. But because I knew the truth. If I gave him those sneakers, it wasn't going to stop. It was going to turn into a habit. From that day on, G-Man never bothered me again.

That's how it was back then. Everything was a test. Every interaction. Every conversation. Every moment where somebody older than you tried to press you. You either passed, or you didn't. And if you didn't pass? You became a mark. Somebody people could take advantage of. But if you did pass? You earned your place. You became part of the circle. And once you're in that circle, it's hard to leave. Because they don't just give you money. They give you identity. They give you purpose. They make you feel like you belong.

I didn't realize it then, but those years—ages thirteen to fifteen—set the course for the rest of my life. The paper routes taught me territory. AJ Lester taught me image. The OJs taught me status. And Preacher, Small Paul, and Mike? They didn't teach me the game. They taught me that in the streets, fear gets you erased. That hesitation costs more than mistakes. That survival isn't about knowing the rules. It's about moving without fear.

CHAPTER 3

BECOMING BONDS

Harlem, 1982-1985
Ages 15-18

My name is Roderick Rowans. But nobody called me that. They called me Bonds. And there's a story behind that name. A story that says everything about who I was trying to become.

I had a best friend named Stan. Stan was my man. We grew up together in Polo Grounds. Same age, same block, same struggles. Me, Stan, and this other cat named Mario—we were tight. The three of us were always together, always into something. Mario ended up doing 25 years. They called him the "brick robber." Said he used to throw bricks out the window of Polo Grounds, hit people in the head, then rob them. I don't know if that's true or not. But that's what they said. Stan ended up doing 25 years too. Federal time. Drug charges. And me? Well, you already know where I ended up. But back then, when we were fifteen, sixteen years old, we were just kids trying to figure out who we wanted to be.

Me and Stan used to go see James Bond movies all the time. Every time a new one came out, we'd hit the theater. We'd watch Sean Connery or

Roger Moore—smooth, sharp, always one step ahead, always getting the girl, always getting out of impossible situations. And Stan would look at me and say, "Yo, that's you, man." "What you talking about?" I'd say. "Nah, for real," he'd say. "You just like James Bond. You stay fresh. You got the girls. You move smooth. You always got a plan."

At first, I thought he was just joking. But he kept saying it. "Yo, little James Bond." "Yo, Bonds." "What's good, Bonds?" And eventually, it stuck. People started calling me Bonds. Not Roderick. Not Rowan. Just Bonds. And I liked it. Because James Bond wasn't just a name. It was an identity. It meant you were sharp. Strategic. Untouchable. It meant you weren't just another kid from the projects. You were somebody.

But here's the thing about identities. Once you put one on, it's hard to take off. Once people start seeing you a certain way, you have to live up to it. And the more I got called Bonds, the more I started acting like Bonds. Cool under pressure. Always ready. Never showing fear. Even when I was scared as hell.

I got my first gun when I was sixteen. I don't even remember exactly how it happened. Somebody gave it to me, or I got it from somebody who knew somebody. That's how it was back then. You didn't have to look hard for a gun in Harlem. If you wanted one, you could get one. And I wanted one. Not because I had enemies. Not because I was in deep yet. But because that's what dudes did. If you were in the streets, you carried a gun. Simple as that. It was part of the uniform. You had your British Walkers, your leather jacket, your fresh haircut—and you had your piece. That's what made you official.

But here's what I didn't understand. I didn't understand that the gun I was carrying wasn't a toy. Wasn't a prop. Wasn't just something to make me look tough. It was a life taker. That's what a gun is. That's what it does. But when you're sixteen years old, you don't think about that. You think about how it feels in your waistband. How it makes you walk differently. How people look at you differently when they know you're strapped. You think about the respect it gets you.

You don't think about the fact that pulling that trigger can end somebody's entire existence. Somebody's mother, father, brother, sister. Somebody's future. Somebody's life. You don't think about the fact that if you use it, your life is over too. You just think: I got this. I'm protected. And you carry it around like it's nothing.

I remember carrying that gun everywhere. To the store. To the block. To see girls. I'd be walking around Polo Grounds with it tucked, acting like everything was normal. And nobody thought twice about it. Because that was normal. That was just how it was. You didn't leave the crib without your gun, the same way you didn't leave without your keys. It became so routine that I forgot how dangerous it was. I forgot that at any moment, I could end up in a situation where I'd have to use it. And once you use it, there's no going back.

School became a joke. I started at Rice High School on 124th Street. Me, Rod Strickland, Jerome Harris—a bunch of us from the neighborhood went there. But I got tired of it. The structure. The uniforms. The rules. So I left and went to my zoned school—Martin Luther King Jr. High School on the Upper West Side. Then I transferred to Brandeis High School. I wasn't going to learn. I was going to be seen.

School wasn't about education for me. It was about status. It was about pulling up in the OJ with my boys, stepping out fly, and letting everybody know we were that crew. We'd get to school late, leave early, and spend most of the day in the cafeteria or the hallways, talking to girls and clowning around. Teachers would try to get us to focus, but we didn't care. Because school wasn't where we were building our futures. The streets were.

I was passing eight classes, though. That's the funny thing. I could've done well if I wanted to. I was smart enough. I just didn't see the point. What was school going to teach me that the streets couldn't? How to get money? The streets taught me that. How to move? The streets taught me that. How to survive? The streets taught me that. School was just something I did because I had to. A formality. A routine. But my real education was happening outside those walls.

By this time, I wasn't just watching the game anymore. I was starting to play it. Not heavy yet. Not like the OGs. But I was dipping my toes in. I'd hold something for somebody. I'd run an errand. I'd be the lookout. And I'd get paid. Not a lot. But enough to keep me moving. Enough to keep me fresh. Enough to feel like I was on my way. And the more I did it, the more I wanted to do it. Because the money was good. The respect was better. And the feeling of being part of something—of being in the circle—was addictive.

But here's what I didn't realize. Every step I took deeper into the streets was a step further away from everything else. Further from my family. Further from any kind of normal future. Further from the version of myself that could've gone a different way. I wasn't thinking about that, though. I was thinking about now. About today. About who I was becoming. Bonds. The name fit. The identity fit. The life fit. And I wore it like a badge of honor.

Polo Grounds was its own world, and we protected it like it was a country. If you didn't live there, you couldn't just walk through. Not without getting checked. "Yo, who you here to see?" "Yo, what building you going to?" If you couldn't answer, you had a problem. And if you were trying to see a girl? You better hope she came downstairs to get you. Because if you thought you were just going to walk up in the building by yourself, you were crazy.

We'd be posted in front, ten, fifteen deep, and we'd stop you. Not because we had anything against you. But because that's how it was. You protected your building. You protected your people. You made it clear that this was ours. I remember girls used to complain about it. "Why y'all always in front of the building? My man don't want to come up here because of y'all." And we'd laugh. "Good. If he scared, he ain't the one."

We thought it was funny. But looking back, I realize we were creating an environment where violence was always just one wrong word away. We were so territorial, so ready to prove ourselves, that even the smallest disrespect could turn into something bigger. And we didn't even realize it. We thought we were protecting the projects. But we were really just trapping ourselves.

I started to notice something around this time. The dudes I looked up to—the ones who had been getting money for years—they were starting to fall. One by one, they were getting locked up. Shot. Killed. Preacher was still around, but he had problems. Police were always on him. Small Paul was moving different. More cautious. Mike? Same thing. The game was changing. Getting more dangerous. More violent. And I was walking right into it.

But I didn't care. Because at sixteen, seventeen years old, you don't think about consequences. You think about now. You think about respect. About money. About being somebody. You think about the name you're building. And I was building mine. Bonds.

Stan used to tell me, "Yo, you gonna be something, man. I can see it. You move different." And I believed him. I thought he meant I was going to make it out. That I was going to be successful. That I was going to be somebody important. But what he really meant was that I was going to be known. And in the streets, being known comes with a price. A price I didn't understand yet. But I was about to find out.

THE WEIGHT OF WHERE YOU'RE FROM

Let me tell you something I wish somebody had told me when I was sixteen. Where you're from doesn't have to be where you end up. I know that sounds simple. Like some motivational poster shit. But hear me out. When I was coming up in Polo Grounds, I thought I only had two choices: be like the dudes who were getting money in the streets, or be invisible. That's it. That's all I saw. I didn't see the third option. The option where I could be somebody without carrying a gun. Where I could have respect without risking my life. Where I could matter without becoming a statistic. Nobody showed me that option. Or maybe they did, and I just wasn't paying attention. Because the truth is, there were people in those same projects who went to school every day. Who graduated. Who got jobs. Who made it out without catching a body or doing time. But I didn't want to be them. I wanted to be Bonds.

THE LESSON I LEARNED TOO LATE

Your environment will try to tell you who you are. It'll tell you that because you're from the projects, you're supposed to struggle. It'll tell you that because your father wasn't there, you're supposed to fail. It'll tell you that because you grew up around violence, you're supposed to be violent. And if you're not careful, you'll believe it. I believed it. I thought being from Polo Grounds meant I had to move a certain way. Talk a certain way. Prove myself a certain way. I thought carrying a gun made me a man. I thought being feared meant being respected. I thought loyalty to the streets was the only loyalty that mattered. And all of that was a lie. But by the time I figured that out, I had already made choices I couldn't take back.

A QUESTION TO SIT WITH

Who are you loyal to, and why? Not who you say you're loyal to. Not who you think you're supposed to be loyal to. But really—who are you protecting, and what is that loyalty costing you? Are you loyal to your boys because they're really your brothers? Or because you're afraid of what happens if you walk away? Are you loyal to the block because it's home? Or because you don't believe you deserve anything better? Are you loyal to a version of yourself that's keeping you stuck?

I was loyal to the streets because I thought that's what made me somebody. But the streets weren't loyal to me. The streets didn't visit me in prison. The streets didn't take care of my family when I was gone. The streets didn't give a damn about me. And if you're reading this right now, the streets don't give a damn about you either. So ask yourself: What are you really protecting?

THE CHOICE POINT

Here's the moment I could've chosen differently. When I got my first gun at sixteen, I had a choice. I could've said no. I could've walked away. I could've realized that carrying a gun didn't make me safer—it made me more likely to use it. But I didn't see it that way. I thought the gun was protection. I thought it was power. And once I had it, I became a different person. I walked different. I talked different. I made decisions I wouldn't have made if I wasn't carrying. And eventually, I used it. That's what guns do. They don't just sit there. They get used. And once you use one, your life is never the same.

So here's the choice point: when somebody offers you a way into the life, you don't have to take it. I know it feels like you do. I know it feels like saying no makes you weak, makes you soft, makes you less than. But saying no is the hardest thing you'll ever do. And it's the only thing that'll save your life.

A WORD FOR THE READER

If you're reading this and you're young—if you're standing where I was standing, trying to figure out who you are, trying to prove yourself, trying to earn respect—I need you to hear this. You don't owe the streets nothing. You don't owe your block nothing. You don't owe the people who are telling you what a man is supposed to be. You owe yourself a future.

I know it feels like the block is all you got. I know it feels like the people around you are the only ones who understand you. I know it feels like leaving makes you a traitor. But staying will kill you. It'll kill you literally—with a bullet, with a prison cell, with a life sentence. Or it'll kill you slowly—with regret, with trauma, with the knowledge that you had a chance to be more and you didn't take it. I'm not saying leave your people. I'm not saying forget where you came from. I'm saying don't let where you came from be the only place you ever go.

You think you're building a reputation. But what you're really building is a cage. A cage made of expectations. A cage made of loyalty to the wrong things. A cage made of trying to prove you're tough enough, hard enough, real enough. And once you're in that cage, it's almost impossible to get out. I know. I spent most of my life in that cage.

I'm 58 years old now, and I'm still dealing with the consequences of choices I made when I was 16. So if I could go back and talk to young Bonds—the kid who thought carrying a gun made him somebody—I'd tell him this: You're already somebody. You don't need a gun to prove it. You don't need the streets to validate it. You don't need to risk your life to earn respect. You just need to choose differently. One choice. One moment. One decision that says, "I'm worth more than this." That's all it takes.

I didn't make that choice. But you still can.

CHAPTER 4

THE FIRST BODY

Harlem, 1986
Age 19

My sister had a boyfriend. Dude was getting a lot of money. Real money. And he wasn't just some random cat from the neighborhood. He was connected. He ran with Gusto and them—dudes from Uptown who owned Rooftop, the skating rink on 155th Street. If you know, you know.

Rooftop wasn't just a skating rink. It was the spot. Every Friday and Saturday night, that's where everybody went. You had people from all over Harlem, the Bronx, Brooklyn, pulling up in their freshest fits, ready to party. And my sister's boyfriend—my brother-in-law, even though they weren't married yet—he was in there every weekend. VIP status.

One day he pulled me to the side. "Yo, Bonds," he said. "I see you out here wilding. I see what you doing. And if you gonna be out here doing that, you might as well do it with me. At least I can look out for you." My sister must've told him about the things I was getting into. The late nights. The money I was making. The risks I was taking. And instead of telling me to stop, he said, Come with me. So I did.

He put me on. We started hustling together. Heavy. He had connects I didn't have. He had money I didn't have. And he brought me in. By this time, I'm 19 years old, and I'm not just dabbling anymore. I'm in it.

Me, my man Estos, and my man June Bug—we opened up a spot on 149th Street between Bradhurst and Eighth Avenue. A little tenement building. My brother-in-law gave us $10,000 worth of crack, and we hit the ground running. At first, I thought we were competing with the other spots in the block. They had twenties, but we came out with nickels. And within two months, our line was around the corner. This taught me that there wasn't any competition. People wanted those nickels. We were moving work faster than anybody expected. And just like that, I was getting money. Real money.

Every Friday and Saturday, we'd close the spot down and go to Rooftop. That was the routine. We'd get fresh, throw on our all-whites or whatever the vibe was that week, and roll deep to 155th. Rooftop was where you went to be seen. To show people you were getting it. To let everybody know you were somebody. And because my brother-in-law was tight with Gusto, we always got in. No problems. No questions. We'd walk through that place like we owned it. Girls everywhere. Music bumping. Everybody trying to outdo each other with their fits, their jewels, their energy. It was the best time of my life. Until it wasn't.

One night, we were outside Rooftop. The night was winding down, and people were starting to leave. My brother-in-law got into it with some dudes. I don't even remember what it was about. Probably nothing. A look. A word. Some disrespect, real or imagined. But that's all it took.

Words were exchanged. Tensions rose. And then my brother-in-law did something I'll never forget. He threw a lollipop at their car. A lollipop.

Just a stupid, childish gesture. A way to say, Fuck you without actually doing anything. But the dude in the car didn't see it that way. He reached down. Into the car. Like he was about to grab something. And I thought, He's going for a gun.

I didn't think. I just moved. I pulled my gun and I let it go. Pop. Pop. Pop. The sound echoed off the buildings. People were screaming. Two people got hit. The guy who reached down in his car died. The other one survived. And just like that, everything changed.

I ran. Not because I thought it through. Not because I had a plan. But because that's what you do when shots are fired and people are dying. You run. I got in the car. We drove off. And my mind was racing, trying to catch up to what just happened. I just shot somebody. I just killed somebody. I just took a life.

But even in that moment, I didn't fully process it. I didn't think about the person's mother. Their family. Their friends. The fact that somebody's son, somebody's brother, somebody's father wasn't coming home tonight. I didn't think about any of that. I just thought: I gotta get out of here.

My brother-in-law and I went to Florida together. We stayed down there for about a month, maybe two. Laying low. Trying to figure things out. Trying to see what life was going to look like next. But money started getting low. So we made the decision to come back to New York to get money again.

That's when everything unraveled. It was a snowy night. One of those winter nights where the streets are quiet but heavy. As I came through the block, I saw Homicide roll past. And anybody from the hood knows this: homicide is the only unit that rides four deep in one car. They followed me for two blocks. Then they jumped out on me.

I didn't have my license on me, so they took me to the precinct. The whole time they kept telling me I was there for my license. But I knew better. Four police don't come get you for a license. Eventually, they let me go. They said whoever the car belonged to could come pick it up. My brother-in-law came.

What we didn't know was that there were 577 tips. And those tips said he was the one who committed the murder. So I walked out free. And he got locked up and charged for something he didn't do. And that left me with one decision to make.

I walked into the precinct and told them, "I did it." The cops looked at me like I was crazy. "You know what you're saying right now?" one of them asked. "Yeah," I said. "I know." They tried to talk me out of it. They told me I was young, that I had my whole life ahead of me, that I should just walk away and live my life. But I couldn't. Because in my mind, loyalty was everything. And if I let my brother-in-law take that charge, I wasn't loyal. I was a coward.

They let my brother-in-law go. And they charged me with murder. I went to the grand jury. My lawyer worked out a deal. Instead of murder, we pled down to manslaughter. Five to fifteen years. I took it. I was nineteen years old.

Here's what I didn't expect. The respect. When word got out that I turned myself in, that I took the charge so my man wouldn't have to, the streets looked at me different. OGs I didn't even know started reaching out to me. Mr. Willie. Tito Johnson. Old Man Carter. They'd see me and say, "Yo, we heard what you did. We ain't seen that type of shit since the 60s." They were talking about the old code. The real code. Where if you did something, you owned it. You didn't let somebody else take your weight. And because I did that, I earned a respect I didn't even know existed.

People who would've never looked twice at me before now knew my name. Bonds. The young boy who turned himself in for a body.

But here's what nobody talks about. That respect came with a price. Because now I wasn't just Bonds, the kid from Polo Grounds who was trying to make a name for himself. I was Bonds, the kid who caught a body. The kid who was willing to do whatever it took. The kid who didn't fold under pressure. And in the streets, once you have that reputation, you can't lose it. You have to live up to it. Every day. Every situation. Every moment where somebody's watching to see if you're really who they say you are.

I was out on bail for two years as I awaited sentencing. And during those two years, I had a lot of time to think. I thought about the person I killed. About his family. About what they must be going through. I thought about my own family. About my mother, my siblings, the people who loved me and didn't want to see me throw my life away. I thought about the choices I made that led me to that moment. The people I followed. The life I chose. The gun I carried without thinking about what it really meant. And I thought about the fact that at nineteen years old, I was facing the possibility of spending the next fifteen years in a cage.

But even with all that time to think, I still didn't fully understand. I still thought this was just part of the game. I still thought I did the right thing by turning myself in. I still thought the respect I earned was worth it. I didn't realize yet that I had just traded my freedom for a reputation. And reputations don't keep you warm at night. They don't visit you in prison. They don't bring you home.

In 1987, I took the plea. Five to fifteen years. Mario Cuomo was the governor back then, and he wasn't as hard on violent crime as the people who came after him. So I got lucky. If this had happened five years later, I would've gotten way more time. But still. Five to fifteen. For a twenty-one-year-old kid, that might as well be a lifetime.

I got sent to Elmira Correctional Facility. And that's where I learned what prison really was. Not the stories. Not the myths. Not the tough-guy talk. The reality. The violence. The politics. The constant need to prove yourself. The boredom. The loneliness. The way time moves so slow that days feel like weeks and weeks feel like years. And the knowledge that every single day you're in there, life is going on without you. People are moving on. Relationships are ending. Opportunities are passing. And you're stuck.

But I also learned something else. I learned that in prison, your name travels faster than you do. By the time I got to Elmira, people already knew who I was. "Yo, that's Bonds. He turned himself in for his man. He's solid." And because of that, I had a certain level of protection. A certain level of respect. OGs looked out for me. People I didn't even know made sure I was good. And that taught me something important. Loyalty—real loyalty—is currency. But it only matters if people know about it.

I served three and a half years. I got work release. Came home in 1990. Twenty-two years old. A convicted felon. A body on my record. But in the streets, I was a legend. And I thought that was a good thing.

CHAPTER 5

THE CAGE

Elmira Correctional Facility, New York
1987

They call it "gladiator school." That's what Elmira was. That's what it is. Not because of the name. Not because of the history. But because when you walk into that place, you better be ready to fight. For your respect. For your safety. For your life. And I walked in there at nineteen years old, thinking I was ready. I wasn't.

The first thing you notice about Elmira is the size. It's massive. 2,500 inmates. And when you're in the gym—which is where everybody goes—there's 1,800 people in there at one time. Eighteen hundred. Imagine walking into a space where damn near two thousand men are sizing you up, trying to figure out who you are, what you're about, and whether you're a threat or a target. That's what I walked into. And I was terrified. Not that I'd show it. But inside? I was terrified.

I got processed through reception. They gave me my uniform, my number, my bunk assignment. And then they told me I was going to max. Maximum security. That meant that jail wasn't going to be a vacation. I was going to be with the violent offenders. The lifers. The dudes who had nothing to lose. When you go to Elmira, if you're classified as max, all they do is open a door from reception to the max unit. You just walk through. And everybody in there already knows you're coming.

I found out later that people were following my story from the streets. They knew I was in reception. They knew I was classified as max. They knew I'd be walking through that door any day. And some of them were waiting for me.

A dude named Pep came to see me before I even hit the yard. Pep was what they called a grievance rep. That meant he could move around the facility freely, checking on inmates, handling complaints, making sure people weren't getting mistreated. But really, Pep was an OG. Somebody the inmates respected. He came to reception and asked for me by name. "Yo, you Bonds?" he said. "Yeah, that's me." "I'm Pep. I'm from Harlem. Heard about you. When you hit the yard tomorrow, come see me." I didn't know what that meant. Was it a good thing? Was I about to get tested? Was he trying to help me or set me up? I didn't know. But I said, "Alright, cool." And he left.

The next day, I went to the yard. And I could feel it. Eyes on me. People watching. Trying to figure out who I was. I walked slow. Didn't look scared. Didn't look tough. Just walked like I belonged there. And then I saw Pep. He waved me over. "Yo, Bonds. We need to talk."

Here's what I didn't know. There was a situation back home involving a dude named Crusher. Crusher was heavy in the streets. He was my brother-in-law's partner. Part of the crew I was hustling with before I got locked up. One day, Crusher came to the block—149th Street—and somebody shot him up. My man Sammy—OG Sammy—ran to the window and saw the whole thing go down. He yelled out, "Yo, Bonds! Yo! That's your man Crusher! Somebody just shot him!" But by the time the story made it to prison, it got twisted. People were saying we did it. That my crew set Crusher up. That I had something to do with it. And Crusher's people? They were in Elmira. Waiting for me.

Pep explained it to me. "Yo, they saying you had something to do with Crusher getting shot. They were gonna move on you as soon as you hit the yard." My heart dropped. "Yo, I didn't have nothing to do with that," I said. "Crusher was my man. We were getting money together. Why would I do that?" Pep looked at me. "I believe you. But you gotta understand—stories get twisted in here. People hear one thing, and by the time it gets around, it's something completely different."

He told me he'd already talked to the people who were planning to move on me. Told them to hold off. Told them he wanted to hear my side first. "I'm gonna go back and straighten this out," he said. "But you need to stay low for a minute. Let me handle it." And he did. Pep went back to Crusher's people and told them the real story. Told them I wasn't involved. Told them it was just some jail shit—rumors, gossip, nothing real. And they backed off. Just like that, the threat was gone.

But that's how prison works. You can get killed over a rumor. Over something you didn't do. Over something somebody said you did. And if you don't have people looking out for you, if you don't have a name that carries weight, you're done. I got lucky. My name had already traveled. People knew I turned myself in. They knew I took a body for my man. They knew I was solid. And because of that, Pep gave me a chance. But not everybody gets that chance.

After that situation got cleared up, I started to settle in. And that's when I realized: I know people in here. One day I'm walking through the gym, and this big dude comes up to me. "Yo, what's up, little Rowan?" I looked at him, trying to figure out who he was. "Yeah, what's up?" I said, cautiously. "Yo, it's me. Big Al." Big Al. I hadn't seen this dude in fifteen years. He liked one of my sisters back in the day, and then one day he just disappeared. Now here he is, standing in front of me in Elmira, looking like he's been here forever. "Yo, what's good, Al?" I said, dapping him up. "Man, I heard you was coming through. You good? You need anything?" And just like that, he handed me my tools. A shank. A blade. A piece of metal sharpened down to a point. "Keep this on you," he said. "You never know when you gonna need it." That was prison. You didn't ask questions. Somebody looked out for you, you took what they gave you and kept moving.

I started seeing more people I knew. Larry Moe from 137th Street in Manhattan. Kim Ben, Do Up's little brother from 158th and St. Nick. Dudes from all over Harlem, the Bronx, Brooklyn. And because my name had respect, they checked on me. Made sure I was good. Made sure I had what I needed. That's the thing about prison. It's dangerous as hell. But if you're connected, if people know you, if your reputation precedes you— it's a different experience. You're still locked up. You're still in a cage. But you're not alone.

The gym was where everything happened. That's where you worked out. Where you played ball. Where you gambled. Where you handled your business. And when I first walked into that gym and saw 1,800 men in there at one time, I thought, This is it. This is the jungle. But then I realized something. It wasn't the jungle. It was a gladiator arena. Everybody in there was trying to survive. Trying to prove themselves. Trying to make it to the next day without getting stabbed, jumped, or worse. And the only way to survive was to be smart. Know who to talk to. Know who to avoid. Know when to stand up and when to walk away. I learned that fast.

The crazy thing about prison is how slow time moves. Days feel like weeks. Weeks feel like months. Months feel like years. You wake up. You eat. You go to the yard. You go to the gym. You go back to your cell. You sleep. And then you do it all over again. Every. Single. Day. There's no variation. No excitement. No freedom. Just routine.

And the routine breaks you down. It makes you forget what life was like on the outside. It makes you forget what you were fighting for. It makes you forget who you are. Some dudes lose themselves completely. They become institutionalized. They can't function anywhere else. I told myself I wouldn't be one of those dudes. I told myself I'd do my time and get out. But deep down, I knew I was changing. I was becoming harder. Colder. More numb. Because that's what you have to do to survive in there. You shut off the part of you that feels. And once you shut it off, it's hard as hell to turn it back on.

I served three and a half years. Got work release. Came home in 1990. I was twenty-three years old. A convicted felon. A body on my record. A reputation that preceded me. And when I hit the streets, people looked at me different. Not with fear. Not with judgment. With respect. "Yo, that's Bonds. He turned himself in. He's solid." And I thought that was a good thing. I thought the respect I earned was worth the time I did.

But what I didn't realize was that respect came with expectations. Now people expected me to move a certain way. To be a certain person. To live up to the reputation I'd built. And once you have that reputation, you can't lose it. You have to keep proving yourself. Over and over and over again.

Prison didn't rehabilitate me. It didn't teach me a lesson. It didn't make me want to change. All it did was make me better at the game. Better at moving. Better at surviving. Better at playing the role. And when I came home, I went right back to what I knew. Because that's all I knew.

BOND CHECK #2

THE PRICE OF PROVING YOURSELF

Let me be real with you. Catching a body doesn't make you a man. Going to prison doesn't make you tough. Turning yourself in doesn't make you a hero. I know the streets will tell you different. I know people will say, "Yo, he kept it real. He stood up. He didn't let his man take the charge." And yeah, that's loyalty. But loyalty without wisdom is just stupidity with a better reputation.

THE LESSON I LEARNED TOO LATE

When I turned myself in for that body, I thought I was doing the honorable thing. And in the streets, I was. People respected me for it. OGs looked at me different. My name rang out. But here's what nobody tells you. That respect doesn't pay your bills. That respect doesn't bring back the person you killed. That respect doesn't give you back the years you lost.

I was twenty-one-years old when I went to prison. I came home at twenty-three. But was on work release for another three and a half years. Three and a half years doesn't sound like a lot but when you add in work release and parole that's close to 15 years of my life down the drain. Also, when you're that young, those are the years you're supposed to be figuring out who you are. Building relationships. Making memories. Learning skills. Creating a foundation for your future. I lost all of that. And for what? So people could say I was solid? So I could have a reputation?

A reputation doesn't visit you in prison. A reputation doesn't cry at your funeral. A reputation doesn't take care of your family when you're gone. It's just a story people tell about you after you're gone.

A QUESTION TO SIT WITH

What are you trying to prove, and who are you trying to prove it to? Think about that. Really think about it. Are you carrying that gun because you need it? Or because you're trying to prove you're not scared? Are you getting into that beef because you have to? Or because you're trying to prove you're not soft? Are you doing dirt because you need the money? Or because you're trying to prove you're built like that?

Most of the time, we're not doing what we're doing because we have to. We're doing it because we're trying to prove something. To our boys. To the block. To the people who doubted us. To ourselves. And that need to prove ourselves will get us killed.

I pulled that trigger because I thought somebody was reaching for a gun. But even if he was—did I have to shoot? Could I have moved different? Could I have walked away? Or was I so deep in the mindset of "I gotta handle this" that I didn't even consider another option? The truth is, I wanted to prove I was that dude. And proving it cost me fifteen years of my life. And cost somebody else their entire life.

THE CHOICE POINT

The moment I could've chosen differently was outside Rooftop that night. When my brother-in-law threw that lollipop at the car, when those dudes reacted, when the tension started building—I had a choice. I could've said, "Yo, let's go. It ain't worth it." I could've pulled my man away from the situation. I could've de-escalated instead of escalated. But I didn't.

Because in that moment, I thought being a man meant being ready to shoot. I thought loyalty meant being willing to kill for my people. I thought walking away made me weak. So I stayed. And I pulled the trigger. And everything after that—the running, the hiding, the turning myself in, the prison time, the reputation—all of it came from that one choice. That one moment where I chose to prove I was willing to go there. And I can't take it back.

A WORD FOR THE READER

If you're reading this from a cell right now—if you're doing time for something you did, something you can't undo—I need you to hear this. You're not your worst decision. I know it feels like you are. I know it feels like that's all people see when they look at you. I know it feels like you'll never be anything other than your charges, your time, your record. But that's not true. You're more than what you did. You're more than the worst moment of your life.

And when you get out—not if, when—you have a choice to make. You can come home and go right back to what you were doing. You can pick up where you left off. You can try to reclaim the reputation you had, the respect you earned, the status you lost. Or you can choose different. You can say, "I paid for what I did. I'm not paying for it for the rest of my life." You can say, "The streets don't own me. My past doesn't define me. I'm building something new."

It won't be easy. People will test you. They'll try to pull you back. They'll say you changed, you went soft, you're not the same. And you're not. Because growth looks like change. And change looks like leaving behind the version of yourself that got you locked up in the first place.

I came home from Elmira thinking I was the same person. But I wasn't. Prison changed me. It made me harder. It made me colder. It made me more willing to do what I had to do to survive. And that mindset followed me for the next thirty years. It followed me into every decision I made. Every relationship I had. Every situation I walked into. Because once you prove you're willing to go to that level, people expect it from you. And you start expecting it from yourself. You start thinking, "This is who I am. This is what I do." And you forget that you ever had a choice.

But you do. You always do. Taking a body doesn't make you a man. Being willing to die for the wrong things doesn't make you loyal. Proving you're tough doesn't make you strong. Real strength is walking away from a fight you know you can win. Real loyalty is protecting the people you love by staying alive, staying free, staying present. Real manhood is being able to look at yourself in the mirror and know that your choices are building something, not destroying it.

I didn't learn that at nineteen. I didn't learn it at twenty-two. I didn't learn it until I was damn near sixty years old, sitting in a doctor's office with a cancer diagnosis, looking back at my life and asking myself: What was it all for? The respect? The reputation? The name? None of it mattered.

What mattered was the time I lost. The people I hurt. The life I could've lived if I'd just chosen different.

You still have time. You still have a choice. Don't waste it trying to prove something that doesn't matter.

PART TWO: THE HUSTLE

CHAPTER 6

COMING HOME

Harlem, 1990
Age 22

I came home on a Tuesday. Work release. Three and a half years served on a five-to-fifteen. I stepped off the bus at the Port Authority, walked through Times Square, caught the train uptown, and when I hit 155th Street, it felt like I'd never left. Same buildings. Same people. Same energy. But I was different. And everybody could see it.

The first person I saw when I got to the block was Old Man Carter. He was sitting on the bench in front of the building, same spot he always sat, watching everything, knowing everything. When he saw me, he stood up. "Bonds," he said. "Welcome home." We dapped up, and he looked at me— really looked at me—like he was trying to see if prison had broken me or made me. He was one to never have a lot of words but looked me dead in the eye and said. "Listen to me, young blood. Shit done changed out here. It ain't the same game no more. These new niggas ain't got no code, no honor. Trust nobody. I mean nobody. The same cats you think you riding for will turn on you in a heartbeat if it means they can save themselves."

He shook his head. "Stay out these streets, Bonds. You beat this case, you got a second chance. Don't waste it chasing the wrong shit." I nodded, told him I heard him. But I didn't listen. If I would've listened to Old Man Carter that day, I wouldn't be in half the shit I ended up in. I wouldn't have spent twenty years protecting a man who saw me as nothing more than help. But back then, I was young. I thought I knew better. I thought loyalty meant something to everybody. I was wrong.

"You solid," he continued. "That means something. Don't forget it." And then he sat back down. That was it. That was the welcome home. But that one conversation set the tone for everything that came after.

People knew my name now. Not just in Polo Grounds. Not just on my block. Everywhere. I'd walk through Harlem, and dudes I didn't even know would nod at me. "Yo, that's Bonds." "Yo, what's good, Bonds?" "Yo, I heard about you. Respect." OGs who wouldn't have looked at me twice before I went in were now pulling me to the side, telling me if I ever needed anything, they had me.

Tito Johnson—who also went by Top—made it a point to check on me. "Yo, Bonds, you need work? You need money? You need anything?" Mr. Willie, another OG from the neighborhood, same thing. "Yo, if you ever in a jam, come see me." I had respect. Real respect. The kind of respect that opens doors. But I was also on parole. And parole meant I needed a job.

I got a job at Taino Towers on 122nd Street. It was one of those big housing complexes on the East Side, and they had an assistant living program on the second floor. I worked there, helping out, doing whatever needed to be done. It wasn't much. But it was legitimate. And being on parole, I needed legitimate. I couldn't afford to get caught slipping. Couldn't afford to get violated and sent back upstate. So I went to work every day. Kept my head down. Did what I was supposed to do. But at night? At night, I was back in the streets.

See, here's the thing about coming home from prison. You come home to the same environment that got you locked up in the first place. Same people. Same blocks. Same temptations. And even if you want to do right, even if you're trying to stay clean, the streets don't let you go that easy. Because everybody knows you. Everybody knows what you're about. And they're watching to see if you're still that dude or if prison changed you.

So you have a choice. You can prove you changed—and risk losing the respect you earned. Or you can prove you're still the same—and risk going right back to prison. I chose the second option.

I started dipping and dabbling again. Nothing too heavy at first. Just a little crack money on the side. Enough to supplement what I was making at the job. Enough to stay fresh. Enough to keep up. Because I wasn't trying to go backwards. I'd been locked up for three and a half years. I'd missed birthdays, holidays, everything. I'd watched life go on without me. And now that I was home, I wanted to make up for lost time. I wanted the money. The clothes. The respect. The feeling of being somebody. And the streets gave me that. The job at Taino Towers? That just kept parole off my back.

In 1992, Riverbank State Park opened. It's this huge park on the West Side, right on the Hudson River. Basketball courts, swimming pools, a skating rink, everything. And they were hiring. I applied and got the job with the Parks Department. It was one of the few places that would hire you even if you had a record. They'd look past your criminal background if you were honest about it. So I worked there. Legitimate money. Benefits. A real job. And I kept hustling at night. Two lives. Two versions of myself.

By day, I was Roderick Rowan, Parks Department employee, trying to do right. By night, I was Bonds, still getting money in the streets, still moving how I'd always moved. And I thought I could balance it. I thought I could have both.

Around this time, my cousin Mike Geronimo started blowing up. Mike was a rapper. A good one. And he'd just signed to Irv Gotti. If you don't know, Irv Gotti—back then people called him DJ Irv—was one of the biggest producers and executives in New York. He was building an empire, and Mike Geronimo was his first artist. Mike had a joint out called "Shit Is Real." It was getting burn. People were talking about him. And Mike looked at me and said, "Yo, Bonds, I want you to roll with me." I didn't even think twice. "Say less."

Mike and I were tight. Our fathers worked together for years and made sure that our families were family. But Mike took a different path. He went the music route. And now he was making moves. And because I'd just come home, because I had a reputation, because people knew I was solid, Mike wanted me around. Not just as security. As his man. His family.

So I started traveling with him. Studio sessions. Shows. Industry events. And that's when I got my first real taste of the music industry. Mike was signed to Irv Gotti, but under Irv was another artist: Ja Rule. This was before Ja Rule was Ja Rule. Before "Holla Holla." Before Murder Inc. became what it became. This was when Ja was just a young cat from Queens trying to make it. And I was around all of them.

I'd be in the studio while Mike was recording. I'd be backstage at shows. I'd also be at meetings, listening to deals being made, watching how the business worked. And I started to see something. The music industry wasn't that different from the streets. Same power dynamics. Same loyalty tests. Same people trying to eat off each other. The only difference was the money was legal.

But I still had one foot in the streets. Because the money from traveling with Mike wasn't consistent yet. And I had bills. I had responsibilities. So I kept hustling. I'd be in the studio with Mike one night, and the next night I'd be on the block moving work. Two worlds. Two lives. And I thought I was winning. I thought I was playing the game smart. Making moves on both sides. Keeping my options open.

But what I didn't realize was that living like that—trying to be in two places at once—was exhausting. And eventually, something was going to give.

People used to ask me, "Yo, Bonds, what you doing? You working at the park. You hustling. You traveling with Mike. Which one is it?" And I'd say, "All of it." Because in my mind, I was hedging my bets. If the music thing didn't work out, I had the streets. If the streets got too hot, I had the job. If the job wasn't enough, I had Mike. I thought I was being strategic. But what I was really doing was refusing to commit to anything. Because committing meant choosing. And choosing meant walking away from something. And I wasn't ready to walk away from the respect I had in the streets.

One night, I'm in the studio with Mike, and Irv Gotti comes through. He looks at me and says, "Yo, you Mike's cousin, right?" "Yeah, that's me." "Bonds, right?" "Yeah." He nods. "I heard about you. You solid." And then he walks away. That was it. That was the whole conversation. But it meant something. It meant my name traveled. It meant people in the industry knew who I was. It meant I had a reputation that reached beyond the streets.

And for a minute, I thought maybe I could make this music thing work. Maybe I could leverage my reputation into something bigger. Maybe I didn't have to choose between the streets and the industry. Maybe I could have both. But deep down, I knew the truth. You can't serve two masters.

You can't be half in, half out. Eventually, you have to choose. And the longer I went without choosing, the more dangerous it got. Because when you're living two lives, you're constantly one mistake away from losing both.

I stayed at Riverbank State Park for about two years. During that time, I kept hustling on the side. I kept traveling with Mike. I kept trying to balance it all. And on the surface, it looked like I had it figured out. I had a job. I had money. I had respect. I had opportunities. But inside, I was torn. Torn between the life I was trying to leave behind and the life I kept running back to. Torn between doing right and doing what I knew. Torn between who I was and who I was trying to become. And that internal conflict—that constant back and forth—was eating me alive.

Looking back now, I see that period for what it was. A crossroads. I could've walked away from the streets completely. I could've focused on the job, on building something legitimate, on supporting Mike's career and maybe finding my own path in the industry. I had the opportunity. I had people around me who believed in me. I had a second chance. But I didn't take it. Not because I couldn't. But because I wasn't ready.

I wasn't ready to let go of the identity I'd built. I wasn't ready to let go of the respect I'd earned. I wasn't ready to be anything other than Bonds. And that decision—that refusal to choose—set me on a path that would lead me deeper into the streets. Deeper into the game. Deeper into a life I thought I could control.

But nobody controls the streets. The streets control you. And I was about to find that out the hard way.

CHAPTER 7

BALTIMORE RUN

Harlem/Baltimore, 1985-1987
Ages 18-20

Before the body. Before Elmira. Before everything changed. There was Baltimore.

Let me back up. When I was about 18, my sister's boyfriend pulled me in deeper than I'd ever been before. He was getting real money. Not game room money. Not paper route money. Real money. And he was connected to some serious people. Gusto and them—the dudes who owned Rooftop. The dudes who were moving major weight and had the whole uptown scene on lock. My sister's boyfriend saw me out in the streets, saw me trying to figure it out on my own, and he told my sister, "Yo, your little brother's out here wilding. If he's gonna be out here doing that, he might as well do it with me so I can look out for him." And that's how it started.

Around the same time, I linked up with two cats: Estos and June Bug. These dudes were from Uptown, always running around the tenement buildings, always looking for a move. One day I said to them, "Yo, if I get some work, you think we could work out of one of these tenement build-ings?" Estos looked at me and said, "I know we could. I got a building." That same night, my sister's boyfriend gave us $10,000 worth of crack. Ten thousand dollars. At 18 years old. We took that work and opened up a spot on 149th Street, right between Bradhurst and Eighth Avenue. And just like that, I was in the game. For real this time.

But before we got to 149th Street, I spent time in Baltimore. That's where the real education happened. My sister's boyfriend had connects down there. He had a whole operation. And he was working with some heavy hitters from the Bronx. Two brothers: Pretty Ty and Omar. They worked for Crusher. Pretty Ty was the older one. The boss. The one getting all the money. Omar was his little brother. Wherever Ty went, Omar went. Ty kept him close, kept him protected, kept him learning the game. And me? I was down there with them, hustling every day, learning how the drug game really worked.

Baltimore in the mid-80s was different from New York. In New York, you had so much competition that you had to be strategic. You had to know your territory, know your customers, know when to move and when to lay low. But in Baltimore? It was wide open. The fiends were everywhere. The money was fast. And if you knew what you were doing, you could eat. We were eating. Me and Pretty Ty would be out there every single day, moving work, collecting money, re-upping, and doing it all over again. And then we'd come back to New York, lay low for a minute, and head right back down to Baltimore. It became a routine. A profitable routine.

Pretty Ty taught me a lot. He taught me how to move weight. How to deal with different types of customers. How to handle money. How to stay under the radar. But more than that, he taught me how to carry myself. Pretty Ty wasn't loud. He wasn't flashy. He wasn't trying to prove anything to anybody. He was just about his business. And people respected him for it. I wanted to move like that. Quiet. Confident. Respected.

But then everything changed. One day, Pretty Ty got killed. Shot. Gone. Just like that. I don't even remember all the details. Just that one day he was here, and the next day he wasn't. And Omar? Omar lost it. His big brother—the person who kept him grounded, the person who kept him on track—was gone. And Omar didn't know how to handle it. He started wilding out. Getting into trouble. Moving reckless. And eventually, he got locked up and sent to Rikers Island.

That's when everything shifted. Omar went to Rikers and started the Bloods. Not by himself. But he was one of the main ones. One of the founders. The United Blood Nation. UBN. And it spread like wildfire. Within months, the Bloods were all over Rikers. Then all over New York. Then all over the east coast. And it all started because Omar lost his brother and needed a new family. A new structure. A new purpose. The Bloods gave him that.

I didn't see Omar much after that. We crossed paths one night in 2010, briefly. He was on the run. I could tell. We said what's up, kept it short, and kept it moving. Because by then, he wasn't just Omar anymore. He was OG Mack. A legend in the streets. An early architect of the Blood movement in New York. And I was just Bonds, trying to survive my own path.

But back in 1985, before all of that, we were just young dudes trying to get money. Hustling in Baltimore. Learning the game. Thinking we had it figured out. And when Pretty Ty died, it was a reminder that this life didn't come with guarantees. You could be on top one day and gone the next. You could be getting money, living good, thinking you were untouchable—and then a bullet ends it all. But I didn't process that lesson the way I should have. I didn't think, This could be me. I thought, I'm built different. That won't happen to me. And I kept moving.

When I came back to New York full-time, I put all my focus into the spot on 149th Street. We had $10,000 worth of crack. We had a building. We had a plan. And we had ambition. Preacher's man Terry had a spot right on the corner. They'd been there for years. Everybody knew them. Everybody bought from them. They were selling twenties. Big pieces. Big money. But we came in with a different strategy. We came in with nickels.

At first, people thought we were crazy. "Y'all selling nickels? Y'all not gonna make no money off that." But we knew something they didn't. Not everybody had twenty dollars. Not everybody wanted to spend that much at once. But everybody had five dollars. The fiends. The workers. The people just trying to get a little something to get through the day. They all had five dollars. And they all came to us.

Within two months, our line was around the corner. Literally. Around the corner. We had people waiting. People calling ahead. People asking when we were opening, when we were re-upping, when we were coming back. And Terry and them? They had to adjust. They started selling tens. Then they started selling nickels too. Because we'd changed the game on them. We'd shown them that you don't have to sell big to make big money. You just have to sell smart.

I remember one day, I saw Preacher's man Shaft on the corner. He looked at me and shook his head. "Yo, how you just gonna open up like that?" he said. I shrugged. "It's a free country." He laughed. "Man, y'all ain't gonna make no noise with them nickels." But two months later, when our line was wrapped around the block, Shaft wasn't laughing anymore.

And Terry? Terry knew. He knew we were serious. He knew we weren't just some kids playing around. He knew we were a problem.

The crazy thing is, I had respect for Terry. Even though we were competing, even though we were taking his customers, I respected him. Because he was a real one. He'd been in the game for years. He'd built something. And he wasn't a hater. He didn't come at us sideways. He didn't try to shut us down. He just adjusted his game and kept moving. That's the mark of a real player. He didn't get emotional. He got strategic. And I learned from that. I learned that competition is part of the game. And if you're good, you don't need to tear down the next man. You just need to be better.

By 1986, I was 19 years old, and I was getting real money. Not just surviving. Not just getting by. I was eating. I had fresh clothes. A car. I had jewelry. I had respect. I had a crew. I had everything I thought I wanted. And I thought I was untouchable. I thought I'd figured it out. I thought I was smarter than the dudes who came before me. I thought I could navigate the game without getting caught, without getting killed, without going to jail. I thought wrong.

Every weekend, we'd shut down the spot and go to Rooftop. That was the routine. That was the reward. Hustle all week. Party all weekend. And Rooftop was the place to be. Because my sister's boyfriend was tight with Gusto, we always got in. No problems. No questions. We'd pull up in our best fits, walk through like we owned the place, and enjoy the night. Girls. Music. Energy. Freedom. For a few hours every Friday and Saturday, we weren't hustlers. We weren't criminals. We weren't looking over our shoulders. We were just young dudes having fun.

But the streets don't let you have fun for long. The streets always find you.

And one night in 1986, the streets found me outside Rooftop. That night changed everything. That night, I pulled the trigger. That night, I went from being Bonds the hustler to Bonds the killer. And everything I'd built in Baltimore, everything I'd built on 149th Street, everything I thought I had figured out—it all came crashing down.

Because when you live this life, it doesn't matter how smart you are. It doesn't matter how strategic you are. It doesn't matter how much money you're making or how much respect you have. Eventually, the game catches up to you. And when it does, it takes everything.

CHAPTER 8

THE CONFRONTATION

Harlem, 1986-1987
Age 19

S uccess brings attention. And in the streets, attention brings problems. We were doing numbers on 149th Street. The spot was jumping. Money was coming in. And everybody knew it. Including the police.

One day, the cops ran up in the building. They were looking for drugs. Looking for guns. Looking for whatever they could find to justify an arrest. But here's the thing: they got the apartments mixed up. See, Terry and them had a spot right across the street from where we were working. But the police thought our spot was theirs. So when they ran up, they kicked in the wrong door. Terry's door. And they took $1,500. Just took it. No arrest. No paperwork. Just took the money and left.

I didn't think much of it at first. That wasn't my problem. That was between Terry and the Cops. A few days later, I saw Preacher on the block. He walked up to me. "Yo, Bonds," he said. "You got little niggas out here making noise. Police ran up in Terry's spot thinking it was yours. You owe us $1,500." I looked at him like he was crazy. "Yo, Preacher," I said. "I don't owe ya'll nothing. They ran up in your spot, not mine." He stared at me. "Man, you owe me $1,500." "I don't owe you nothing." We left it at that. But I could tell—this wasn't over.

A few weeks later, I saw him again at the Rucker. The Rucker Park tournament. Everybody went there. It was the place to see and be seen during the summer. I was there with my boys, just chilling, watching the game. And then I saw Preacher walking toward me. "Yo, Bonds," he said. "What's up, man? You got my money?" "Man," I said, trying to keep it cool. "I don't owe you no money." He looked at me. Didn't say anything. Just looked at me. And then he walked away. But I knew what that look meant. It meant this was building. It meant he wasn't letting it go. It meant sooner or later, we were going to have a real problem.

About two weeks later, I'm standing on the corner of 152nd and Eighth Avenue. It's the middle of the day. Sun is out. People everywhere. I got my car parked sideways—my 1986 Volkswagen Jetta. Had the burgundy one. That was the car back then. Everybody wanted a Jetta. I'm talking to this girl, just kicking it, not thinking about nothing. And then I see him. Three blocks away. Bow-legged walk. I can see it from a distance. Preacher. Walking straight toward me.

My heart started racing. I knew what this was. This wasn't a conversation. This was a confrontation. I could've got in my car and pulled off. I could've walked away. I could've avoided the whole thing. But I didn't. Because walking away meant I was scared. And if I showed fear, I'd lose everything I'd built. The respect. The reputation. The name. So I stayed.

As he got closer, I kept talking to the girl like everything was normal. But inside, I was panicking. Damn. This nigga really coming to the block. When he got close enough, he tapped me on the shoulder. "Yo, Bonds," he said. "49th Street. Now." 49th Street was my block. He was telling me to meet him there. And I knew—if I didn't go, I'd look like a coward. But if I did go, I might not come back.

I looked at the girl, played it cool. "Alright, cool," I said to Preacher. I got in my car. And I drove to 49th Street. The whole way there, my mind was racing. What is he gonna do? Is he gonna shoot me? Is he gonna jump me? Is he bringing niggas with him? But I kept driving. Because that's what you do. You don't run. You face it.

When I pulled up to 49th Street, Preacher was already there. His man Terry was with him. Terry was another dude from back in the day. Solid. Respected. Dangerous. And across the street, I could see Rich Porter and them standing in front of the pharmacy. Rich Porter. If you know, you know. One of the most legendary dudes from Harlem in the 80s. Before he got killed. Before Alpo. Before all of that. Rich and his crew were just standing there, watching. They weren't involved. But they were paying attention. Because they wanted to see how this played out. They wanted to see if I was really who people said I was.

I got out the car. Preacher and Terry walked up on me. My beeper started going off. I looked across the street. My little mans and them were over there, watching. Strapped. Ready. They were sending me a message: Say the word and we blasting. But I knew—this wasn't a blasting situation. These weren't random dudes. These weren't young boys trying to prove something. This was Preacher. This was Terry. These dudes were strategic. These dudes were connected. If we started shooting, they weren't just gonna shoot back. They were gonna come for everybody. My mother. My father. My family. Everybody. This wasn't about guns. This was about respect.

I stood there, one leg on the sidewalk, one leg on the street. And my leg was shaking. Not visibly. But I could feel it. My whole body was tense. My nerves were shot. But I kept my face calm. Kept my voice steady. Preacher looked at me. "Yo, Bonds," he said. "What's up with that $1,500 you owe me?" "Yo, Preacher," I said. "I told you. I don't owe you nothing. The police ran up in your spot, not mine." His man Terry stepped forward. "Man, you think this is a game?" Terry said. "You know who you talking to?" I looked at Terry. Then back at Preacher. "I know exactly who I'm talking to," I said. "But I ain't owe him nothing. That wasn't my fault."

Preacher stared at me for a long moment. And then he said something I'll never forget. "Yo, Bonds," he said. "If I wasn't so clean right now"—he had a suit on, all dressed up—"I'd punch you in your face." That was it. That was the moment. If I backed down, if I apologized, if I showed any sign of weakness—I was done. But if I stood up, if I held my ground, there was a chance this could go a completely different way.

My leg was still shaking. But I looked him dead in the eye. "Yo, Preacher," I said. "I ain't gonna let you just punch me in my face." Silence. Terry looked at Preacher. Preacher looked at me. And for a second, I thought this was about to turn into something I couldn't come back from. But then Preacher smiled. Just a little bit. Not a friendly smile. But a smile that said, Alright. I see you. "Yeah," he said. "We gonna see." And then they walked away.

I stood there for a minute, watching them leave. My heart was pounding. My hands were shaking. But I didn't move. I waited until they were gone. And then I got in my car and drove back to my apartment.

For the next two weeks, I was stressed the fuck out. I didn't know what was coming. I didn't know if Preacher was gonna send somebody at me. I didn't know if they were gonna run up on me in the middle of the night. I was living in Dunbar at the time—Dunbar Houses on 150th Street. And Dunbar was tricky. Too many turns. Too many places for somebody to hide. So every night, I'd come home late, gun in my hand, checking every corner, every hallway, every shadow. I couldn't sleep. I couldn't relax. I kept thinking, This is it. This is how it's gonna end.

And then one night, my brother-in-law came to see me. I was in SNS on 145th Street, in the back, gambling with some dudes. He walked in and said, "Yo, Bonds, come here." I walked over. "Yo," he said. "Why you didn't tell me you had a beef with Preacher?" "How you know about that?" I asked. "Man, because I just left that nigga," he said. "He told me it's squashed." "It's squashed?" "Yeah. It wasn't like no real paper anyway. He said it was $1,500. I told him you ain't got it." I looked at him. "So how you squash it?" He smiled. "You want to know what I told him?" "Yeah."

"I told Preacher," he said, "'You got too many problems in the street to be worrying about one of them little niggas. One of them little niggas might run up on you with a hoodie on and be the one that gets you.'" I stared at him. "You said that?" "I swear to God, that's what I told him." I couldn't believe it. "What he say?" My brother-in-law started laughing. "He started laughing. Said, 'Man, tell that nigga it's dead. It's over.'"

And just like that, it was squashed. Not because I paid him. Not because I backed down. But because I stood up. And because my brother-in-law—who Preacher respected—put it in perspective. Preacher had bigger problems. Real problems. People in the streets who wanted him dead. And wasting time on some young kid over $1,500 wasn't worth it.

After that, me and Preacher had a different relationship. We weren't friends. But we had respect. Mutual respect. He'd see me on the block and nod. "What's good, Bonds?" "What's good, Preacher?" And that was it.

One time, he even pulled up and gave me and some of my boys a ride. We were meeting on 155th, and he saw me walking and said, "Yo, get in. I'll drop you off." I hesitated for a second. Because in the back of my mind, I was thinking, Is this a setup? But I got in anyway. And he dropped me right off. No drama. No problems.

Before I went to jail, Preacher pulled me to the side one more time. "Yo, Bonds," he said. "You know what your problem is?" "What?" "You make money, and you spend money too fast," he said. "You see this?" He pointed to his wrist. "This the only watch I got. You see Terry? That's the only car he got. But if you came to my house, I got money stacked to the wall."

I listened. "Man, you going away tomorrow, right?" he said. "Yeah." "If you got any problems when you get up there, call me," he said. "You know the phone number to the pay phone on the block. Call it. I'll make sure you're good." And then he said something I'll never forget. "You know what, Bonds?" he said. "Niggas say what they want to say about me. But if a nigga gonna give you some money, ain't you gonna take it?" "Yeah." "So I'm not pressing up on niggas who won't come back at me. I'm pressing up on niggas that's gonna give me their paper. And when you need me, I get paid to handle your problem. You don't got to worry about it." He dapped me up. "But you gotta calm down, man. You moving too fast. You gonna burn out."

He was right. I was moving too fast. Spending too much. Trying to prove too much. And it was about to catch up to me.

But in that moment, standing there with Preacher, I felt like I'd earned something real. Not just respect from the young dudes. But respect from the OGs. The ones who'd been in the game for years. The ones who knew how it really worked. And that respect meant something. It meant I'd passed a test. It meant I was solid. It meant I wasn't just another kid from the projects trying to act tough. I was somebody.

But being somebody came with a price. And I was about to pay it.

CHAPTER 9

THE FEDERAL CASE

Harlem/Federal Prison, 1995-2000
Ages 28-33

I thought I was done with prison. I came home in 1990. Did my time. Paid my debt. Got my life back on track. I had a job, I was traveling with Mike Geronimo, staying low-key, staying smart, staying out of trouble. Or so I thought. The thing about the streets is this: even when you're not in them, they can still pull you back in. And in 1995, they pulled me back in.

It started with a phone call. My man Stan, the same Stan who gave me the name Bonds, had a younger brother named Steve. Steve was getting heavy money in Ohio, moving weight, really eating, until the feds grabbed him. And when the feds lock you up, they don't just want you. They want everybody connected to you. One day Steve called me from jail. He needed help. Some dudes from 140th Street had run off with eight keys from his girl while he was locked up, and the plug was now pressuring her, telling her if she didn't start sleeping with him it would be a problem. He asked me to check it out, just make sure she was good.

I should've said no. I should've stayed out of it. But Steve was my man's little brother, and in the streets loyalty means you show up. What I didn't know, what Steve didn't tell me, was that the feds were listening to every single call. And the moment I agreed to help, they had me. Not for selling drugs. Not for moving anything. For a phone call. Telephone conspiracy. In federal court, talking about a crime is enough.

When Steve's girl told me who the plug was, I almost laughed. His name was Joe Lips. I already knew him. A week earlier, I'd fought him on 129th and Fifth after he tried to talk to my man's baby mother. We scrapped right on the corner. I threw his keys five blocks up the avenue. Only afterward did someone tell me who he really was. The plug. The connect everybody used.

So when I went to meet Joe Lips about Steve's situation, it wasn't hostile. He wasn't on revenge time. We squashed the fight, talked through the eight keys, and parted ways. I thought that was the end of it. It wasn't. Weeks later the feds came for me. Arrested me. Charged me with telephone conspiracy. They didn't even really want me. They wanted Joe Lips. They wanted me to flip. I wouldn't.

My lawyer told me the charge carried zero to five years. If I fought it and lost, I'd get the max. If I took the deal, maybe less. But I knew how this would go. My past was going to walk into that courtroom with me. The body. The state time. The reputation. I took the plea. And the judge did exactly what I expected. He gave me the maximum. Five years. Not for what I did this time, but for everything I'd done before.

Federal prison is different from state. In state, you're around people from your area, people who know the code. In the feds, it's everybody from everywhere. And you do all your time. I got five years and did five years. No shortcuts. No early release.

Being in federal prison exposed me to a different level of thinking. Bigger operations. Bigger connections. People running things from inside. I learned how to think broader, how to see opportunity. I also met people connected to the music industry, managers, producers, artists. And I started to see a path. A way to leverage my experience without risking my freedom.

I had a lot of time to think. About the body. About the years lost. About the phone call that cost me five more. About my family. About the fact that I was going to be thirty-three when I got out and still had nothing solid to show for it. Just a name. Just respect. And I realized that wasn't enough.

Still, I didn't fully change. I still believed I could outthink the system. When I came home in 2000, I told myself I wasn't going back to the block, wasn't selling drugs, wasn't repeating the same mistakes. I wanted another way.

That's when Loon came back into my life. We grew up together. This wasn't industry, this was history. When he got signed to Bad Boy, the attention came fast. Good attention and dangerous attention. He needed someone he could trust. Someone solid. I started moving with him quietly. Backstage. Studios. Shows. Watching rooms, watching people. I wasn't loud. I wasn't chasing visibility. I was just present.

People started noticing. Paul saw me around. Nick put my name in the conversation. By the time introductions happened, recognition was already there. Then came the night at Madison Square Garden. R. Kelly.

Jay-Z. Ty Ty spraying mace. Chaos everywhere. I moved instinctively, protected my people, got them out. I wasn't thinking about opportunity. I was thinking about responsibility.

Not long after, I was offered the job. Head of security for Bad Boy. The golden ticket. The opportunity I thought everything had been leading toward.

What I didn't know was how much that opportunity was going to cost me.

BOND CHECK #3

THE ILLUSION OF LOYALTY

L et me tell you something nobody wants to admit.
Loyalty without boundaries will destroy you.
I learned that the hard way.

When Steve called me from jail, I didn't hesitate. I didn't ask questions. I didn't think about the fact that the feds had him and every call was being recorded. I just said yes. Because in the streets, that's what loyalty looks like. Your man calls. You show up.

What I didn't understand was this: Steve wasn't calling me because he trusted me. He was calling me because he was cooperating. Whether he meant to or not, he was setting me up. And I went to federal prison for five years because I answered a phone call.

That's the part nobody talks about.

THE QUESTION I SHOULD'VE ASKED

Who are you protecting who wouldn't protect you?

Steve was my man's little brother. I wanted to help him. But when the feds came, he didn't protect me. He didn't say, "Bonds had nothing to do with this." He let them build the case. He let me take the hit. And I don't even blame him. When pressure comes, most people protect themselves.

I blame myself for not seeing it.

Because here's the real truth about loyalty in the streets. It usually flows one way. Up. You're loyal to the OG. The boss. The connect. The person with power. But when it's time to pay the price, you're the one paying it. You take the charge. You take the time. You sit in the cell while they stay free.

That's not loyalty. That's exploitation.

Real loyalty is mutual. It's reciprocal. It's both people willing to put skin in the game. And most of the time, that's not what you're dealing with.

THE CHOICE POINT

The moment I could've chosen differently was the phone call. I should've said no. I should've said, "I can't get involved in that." I should've protected myself.

But saying no felt like betrayal. It felt like abandoning my man. It felt like being disloyal. And that feeling cost me five years of my life. Five years I'll never get back. Five years away from my family. Five years in a federal cage.

All because I didn't want to say no.

A WORD FOR YOU

If someone asks you to do something that puts your freedom at risk, hear me clearly. You don't owe them that. I don't care if it's your best friend. Your family. Someone you grew up with. If what they're asking can send you to prison, you have to think about yourself.

That's not selfish. That's survival.

Because the person asking you to take that risk is thinking about their problem, not your future. And if you go down helping them, they're going to keep moving. You'll be the one sitting in a cell asking yourself why you said yes.

I've seen it a thousand times. Somebody's girl gets caught with work and you claim it. Somebody asks you to hold something and you do it. Somebody calls you from jail and asks you to handle something and you jump. Next thing you know, you're in cuffs. Facing years. Losing your life.

All for loyalty that wasn't returned.

THE HARD TRUTH

Your man's case is not your case.

Say it again.
 Your man's case is not your case.

Unless you were there, unless you did it, unless it's truly yours, don't make it yours. I'm not telling you to snitch. I'm not telling you to cooperate. I'm telling you not to put yourself in a position where that choice even exists.

Don't answer jail calls asking you to do dirt.
Don't get involved in problems that aren't yours.
Don't be loyal to people who would let you take their charge.

Because loyalty without wisdom is just stupidity with pride attached to it.
And prisons are full of loyal fools.

I was one of them.

I did five years in federal prison for loyalty. When I came home, nobody was waiting with gratitude or compensation. Steve was free, living his life. And I was starting over at thirty-three with another record and nothing to show for it but a reputation for being solid.

That reputation didn't pay my bills. Didn't take care of my family. Didn't give me back my time. It just made me feel good about myself.

If I could go back to 1995, I'd tell myself this:
When that phone rings, don't answer it. Or answer it and say no. Stand firm. Because five years from now, you'll be sitting in a federal cell while the person you were loyal to is free.

Loyalty is powerful.
But only when it's mutual.
Only when it protects both people.

Most street loyalty doesn't.
It just decides who's going to prison.

And too often, it's you.

ACT II: THE INNER CIRCLE

PART THREE: BAD BOY LIFE

CHAPTER 10

THE DOOR OPENS

New York, 2000
Age 32

I came home from federal prison in the summer of 2000. Thirty-two years old. Two bids under my belt. No money. No car. No job. But I had connections. And in this world, connections are everything.

The first person I went to see was my man Big Dave. Big Dave was from downtown. We'd met years ago at the boat rides and bus trips that Ferg and Def and Rich used to throw back in the day. Those trips to Bear Mountain, the party buses—that's where a lot of us from different parts of the city linked up. Me and Dave got tight. And when I went to the feds, he told me, "Yo, when you come home, come see me." So I did.

Dave was doing his thing. He wasn't in the streets heavy anymore, but he was connected. He knew people. He had access. "Yo, Bonds," he said when I came through. "You good? What you need?"

"Man, I just need to figure out my next move," I said. "I can't go back to the block. I can't risk it."

Dave nodded. "I feel you. Let me make some calls. I'll see what I can do." And just like that, he started opening doors for me.

Around the same time, my man Big Nick came home. Nick was from Polo Grounds. We grew up together. Same block, same projects, same struggles. But Nick had done time for a body too. And when he came home, he started working security. For Puff. Sean "Puff Daddy" Combs. Bad Boy Records. Nick was part of Puff's security team, and he was doing well. Traveling. Making money. Seeing the world.

When I saw him, he told me, "Yo, Bonds, you should get into this."
"Into what?" I asked.
"Security. Entertainment security. You're built for it. You got the respect. You got the experience. And you move the right way."

I thought about it. Security wasn't something I'd ever considered before. But it made sense. I couldn't go back to hustling. I couldn't risk another bid. But I still needed to eat. And if I could get into the industry—travel, make money, be around something bigger—maybe that was the move.

Nick introduced me to Paul, Diddy's head of security. "Yo, Bonds is my man from Uptown," Nick told him. "He solid. He just came home. If you need somebody with you, he's the one." Paul looked at me, sized me up.
"Aight, cool," he said. "Let's rock."
And just like that, I was Paul's personal driver.

At first, it was low-key. Studio sessions. Small shows. Local events. But I was good at it. I knew how to move. I knew how to read a room. I knew when something was about to pop off and how to get ahead of it. And Paul noticed.

"Yo, Bonds, you different," he said one day. "You don't move like regular security. You move like you've been doing this."

"I've been doing a lot of things," I said.

He laughed. "Yeah, I can tell."

Being around Paul gave me access to Bad Boy. Not to Puff yet. But to the world. The studios. The parties. The people. And that's when I started to see it. The music industry wasn't that different from the streets. Same power dynamics. Same hierarchy. Same loyalty tests. The only difference was the money was legal. And the stakes were higher. In the streets, if you mess up, you go to jail or you get killed. In the industry, if you mess up, you lose access. You lose your position. You lose your livelihood. But the game is the same. And I knew how to play the game.

One night, Paul called me.

"Yo, Bonds, I don't feel like going to this event tonight. I need you to roll with Puff. You down?"

"Where we going?" I asked.

"Madison Square Garden. Jay-Z and R. Kelly concert."

I paused. Madison Square Garden. Puff. Jay-Z. R. Kelly. That wasn't just any event. That was major.

"Yeah, I'm down," I said.

"Aight, bet. Meet me in front of Bad Boy."

That night changed my life. I already told you what happened in the prologue. The chaos. The pepper spray. Me getting Ty Ty out of there. Me getting Puff out of there. The whole thing. But what I didn't tell you was what happened after.

When we got back to the studio—Daddy's House—Puff pulled me to the side.

"Yo," he said. "What's your name again?"

"Bonds."

"Bonds," he repeated. "Where you from?"

"Harlem. Polo Grounds."

He nodded. "You just came home, right?"

"Yeah. Did five years federal."

"For what?"

"Conspiracy. Phone charge. Nothing major."

He looked at me for a long moment, like he was trying to figure me out. And then he said, "Yo, you moved right tonight. A lot of niggas would've panicked. But you just moved. You got Ty out. You got me out. You held it down."

"That's what I do," I said.

He nodded again. "Aight. We gonna talk."

Three days later, I got a call from Uncle Paul.

"Yo, Bonds, I need you full-time."

"Full-time?"

"Yeah. Part of the security team when we travel. You good with that?"

I didn't hesitate.

"Yeah, I'm good with that."

Then he told me the details. Sixty thousand a year. Health insurance. Legit paperwork. A real job. And that's when it hit me what this actually was. In the rap game, there were only a handful of people who could afford full-time security year-round. Dr. Dre. Jay-Z. 50 Cent. Puff. Everybody else pieced it together. You worked a tour here, a few dates there, then figured out how to survive in between. Security work wasn't steady. Most guys had to hustle on the side just to stay afloat.

This was different. This meant consistent pay. It meant benefits. It meant not having to scramble for the next gig. For someone like me, coming home after doing time, trying to stay clean and legit, that mattered. A lot. I wasn't being named head of security. I was joining a team. But it was a real opportunity. The kind that didn't come around often. The kind you didn't overthink. So when Paul finished explaining how it worked, I already knew my answer. I said yes.

At the time, it felt like stability. Like progress. Like I'd finally found a way to use what I knew without risking my freedom. What I didn't realize was that full-time access came with full-time expectations. And that some benefits cost more than money.

Paul broke it down for me. The security team at Bad Boy wasn't just regular security. It was a mix. You had ex-cops. Dudes who used to be on the force but retired or got out. You had corrections officers. Dudes who worked at Rikers or other facilities and knew how to handle people. You had federal agents. Not active, but dudes who had connections and could pull strings if needed. And then you had street dudes like me and Nick. Dudes who came from the hood, who had respect, who knew how to move in situations that regular security couldn't handle.

"Your job," Paul said, "is to be the street nigga. The one who can read the room. The one who can spot a problem before it happens. The one who can handle shit that the cops and the COs can't touch."

"I got you," I said.

"Good. Because Puff is different. He's not like regular clients. He doesn't do nine-to-five. He doesn't sleep regular hours. He's always moving. Always working. And when he moves, you move."

"I'm ready."

"Aight. Welcome to Bad Boy."

The first thing I learned was the call time system. Every night, you'd get a text. It didn't matter if it was 2 a.m. or 6 a.m. You'd get a text with the call time for the next day. The call time was when you needed to be downstairs, ready to go, wherever Puff was staying. If he was in a hotel, you'd be in the lobby. If he was at a house, you'd be outside. If he was at the studio, you'd be there before he got there.

And you didn't show up five minutes before call time. You showed up fifteen minutes before, making sure everything was ready. The driver would be there. The car would be cleaned. The route would be planned. And when Puff came down, you'd open the door, close the door, and get in. No conversation. No small talk. Just work.

At first, Puff didn't speak to me. Not because he was rude. But because that's how he operated. He'd have security around him every day, all day, and he wouldn't say a word to them. For weeks, I'd be in the car with him, driving him from place to place, and he'd just be on his phone, working, doing his thing. And I'd be silent. Watching. Listening. Learning.

I didn't take it personal. I understood. Security comes and goes. People quit. People get fired. People move on. So why invest in a relationship with somebody who might not be there next week? But if you proved yourself—if you showed you were solid, reliable, trustworthy—then he'd start to open up. And that's what I did. I proved myself.

The first few months were a test. I'd be at the studio 24 hours a day sometimes. Just sitting there, waiting, in case Puff needed to move. I'd drive him to meetings, to events, to parties, and I wouldn't say a word unless he asked me something. I'd watch how he moved. How he talked to people. How he handled business. I'd watch the people around him. The hangers-on. The yes-men. The people trying to get close. And I'd make sure nothing happened to him.

That was my job. Keep him safe. Keep him moving. Keep him focused.

After about two months, he started speaking to me. Not a lot. But little things.
"Yo, Bonds, you good?"
"Yeah, I'm good."
"You need anything?"
"Nah, I'm straight."

And then one day, after a long session in the studio, he said, "Yo, let's go to Mr. Chow's and eat." That was the signal. That meant I was in. Not just as security. But as somebody he trusted. Somebody he wanted around.

From there, things started to move fast. I went from being the new guy to being one of Puff's main people. I started traveling more. Miami. LA. Atlanta. International trips. And the more I traveled, the more I saw. I saw the parties. The excess. The money. The power. I saw what it meant to be at the top of the industry. And I wanted to be part of it. Not just as security. But as somebody who mattered. Somebody who had a seat at the table.

And for a while, I thought I did.

But there was something I didn't see. Something I didn't understand. Proximity to power is not the same as having power. Being in the room doesn't mean you have a voice. Being close to somebody doesn't mean they're loyal to you.

I didn't see that yet. All I saw was the opportunity. The chance to travel the world. To be around money. To be respected. To be somebody. And I thought that was enough.

But it wasn't.

CHAPTER 11

LEARNING THE SYSTEM

2000-2001
Ages 32-33

There's a system to everything. And working for Puff had a system. A hierarchy. A structure. A way things worked that you had to learn if you wanted to survive. And I learned it fast.

The first thing I learned was about access. Not everybody got the same level of access to Puff. And that access was earned in stages. It was like a graduation.

When I first started, I was staying in hotels. We'd go to Miami, and Puff would stay at his house, and I'd stay at a hotel nearby. The Delano. The Shore Club. Wherever. I'd get the call time texted to me the night before. "7:00 AM - Puff's house." And I'd have to be there at 6:45, waiting outside with the driver, ready to move the second he came out. I'd spend the whole day with him—meetings, studio sessions, events—and then at night, I'd go back to the hotel. That was level one. You were close enough to do your job, but you weren't inside yet.

After a few months, I graduated to the guest house. That meant instead of staying at a hotel, I could stay on the property. Not in the main house, but in the guest house out back. That was a big deal. It meant Puff trusted me enough to have me on the premises. It meant I didn't have to worry about missing a call time because I was stuck in traffic or couldn't get an Uber. I could just walk from the guest house to the main house. And it meant Puff was watching me. Seeing how I moved. Seeing if I respected the space. Seeing if I could be trusted with more access.

After about six months, I graduated to the main house. That meant I could stay in one of the rooms in the main house. Not his room, obviously. But one of the guest rooms. And that was the ultimate level. Because now I was inside. I was part of the inner circle. I was somebody Puff saw every day, all day, and trusted enough to have in his personal space. And with that access came responsibility. Because now I wasn't just security. I was part of the family.

The same graduation system applied to travel. At first, I flew commercial. Delta. American. Whatever. Puff would be on a private jet, and I'd be on a regular flight, meeting him when he landed. But after I proved myself, I started getting put on the manifest for the private jets. And once you're on that manifest, once you're flying private with him, everything changes. Because now you're not just an employee. You're part of the crew. You're sitting on the same plane. Eating the same food. Breathing the same air. And that proximity makes you feel like you're equal. Like you matter. Like you're part of something bigger. But you're not. You're still just security. You're still just an employee. But it doesn't feel that way.

The security team was diverse. You had Uncle Paul, the head of security. He'd been with Puff for years. He knew how everything worked. He was the one who made sure the operation ran smooth. Then you had the ex-cops and the corrections officers. These dudes had badges. They had credentials. They could carry legally in places where we couldn't. If we got pulled over, if we got stopped by security at an event, if something went down—they could flash their credentials and smooth it over. They were the legitimate face of the security team. But they weren't built for certain situations. If things got street, if things got physical, if we had to move in a way that required a different kind of energy—they couldn't do that. That's where me and Nick came in.

We were the street dudes. We didn't have badges. We didn't have credentials. We didn't have the legal protection the cops had. But we had something they didn't have: respect in the streets. If we went to a club in Harlem, in Brooklyn, in Atlanta, in LA—people knew us. Or they knew of us. Or they respected where we came from. And that mattered. Because Puff moved in circles where street credibility mattered. He wasn't just going to corporate events and award shows. He was going to clubs. To parties. To places where the streets and the industry overlapped. And in those places, you needed people who could navigate both worlds. That was us.

But here's the thing about being the street dude on a team like that. You're the most replaceable. The ex-cops? They have skills. Training. Credentials. The COs? Same thing. But street dudes? There's a thousand of us. A thousand dudes who just came home from jail, looking for an opportunity, willing to do whatever it takes to eat. So you had to prove yourself every day. You couldn't slip. You couldn't get comfortable. You couldn't assume your position was secure. Because if you did, you'd be gone. And somebody else would take your spot.

I learned the routine fast. Every night, you'd get a text with the itinerary for the next day. It would have everything. Call time. Locations. Events.

Meetings. Everything. And at the top of the text, in bold, would be the call time. 6:30 AM - The St. Regis Hotel, Lobby. That meant you had to be there at 6:15. Not 6:30. Not 6:25. 6:15. Because if you were on time, you were late. And if you were late, you were done.

The call time was sacred. It didn't matter if you'd been up all night. It didn't matter if you'd just finished a 20-hour day. It didn't matter if you were sick, tired, or hungover. If the call time said 6:30 AM, you were there at 6:15. And you'd wait. Sometimes for five minutes. Sometimes for an hour. Sometimes for three hours. Because Puff operated on his own time. The call time was for you. Not for him. He'd come down when he was ready. And your job was to be ready when he came down.

Most days, Puff wouldn't speak to me in the morning. He'd come down, get in the car, and I'd open the door, close the door, and sit in the front seat. And he'd be on his phone. Working. Texting. Calling. Making moves. And I'd be silent. Just watching. Just waiting. Sometimes he wouldn't say a word to me until 6 or 7 at night. And then, out of nowhere, he'd lean forward and say, "Yo, Bonds, what's good?" And that was the signal. That meant the work part of the day was over. Now we were in the social part. Now we could relax a little. But until he spoke first, you didn't speak. That was the rule.

I started to understand why. Puff was around people all day, every day. Assistants. Managers. Artists. Producers. Engineers. Security. Everybody wanted something from him. Everybody wanted his time, his attention, his energy. And if he let everybody talk to him whenever they wanted, he'd never get any work done. So he controlled access. Even to the people closest to him. And that control extended to conversation. If he wanted to talk, he'd talk. If he didn't, you stayed quiet. It wasn't personal. It was survival.

But here's what I didn't realize at the time. That control—that withholding of attention, of conversation, of acknowledgment—was also a manipulation tactic. Because when he did finally speak to you, when he did finally give you that attention, it felt like a reward. It felt like you'd earned something. And that made you want to work harder. Made you want to prove yourself more. Made you want to be in his good graces. It was brilliant, really. And I fell for it every time.

The workdays were long. I'm talking 18, 20, sometimes 22 hours. You'd start at 6:30 in the morning, and you wouldn't finish until 2 or 3 in the morning the next day. And then you'd get a text at 4 AM with the call time for later that morning. 9:00 AM - Studio. And you'd have to be there. It didn't matter that you'd just worked 20 hours. It didn't matter that you'd only gotten three hours of sleep. You had to be there.

But here's the thing that kept me going. Puff was working those same hours. He wasn't sitting back, relaxing, while we did all the work. He was in the studio for 20 hours. He was in meetings for 12 hours. He was on the phone for 15 hours. He worked harder than anybody I'd ever seen. And that made it easier to accept. Because you'd think to yourself, If he can do 20 hours, I can do 20 hours. You'd see him grinding, pushing, building, and you'd think, This is what it takes to be great. And you'd keep pushing.

But what I didn't realize was that we weren't getting paid the same. He was making millions. I was making $75,000 a year. He was building an empire. I was just working for one. He was creating generational wealth. I was living paycheck to paycheck. But I didn't see it like that at the time. I just saw the proximity. The access. The opportunity. And I thought that was enough.

One day, Puff pulled me to the side. We were in Miami. We'd just finished a long day—meetings, studio time, appearances—and we were sitting by the pool. "Yo, Bonds," he said. "I need to tell you something." "What's up?" I said.

"You're not gonna make a lot of money working for me," he said. "Not right away. But you're gonna be rich in relationships."

I looked at him, not sure what he meant. "When you're with me," he continued, "you're gonna meet everybody. Producers. Artists. Executives. Billionaires. And if you play it right, if you move smart, those relationships will change your life." He paused. "But you gotta be patient. You gotta build. You gotta earn trust. And over time, those relationships will be worth more than whatever I'm paying you." I nodded. It made sense. And I believed him.

But here's what he didn't say. Those relationships only mattered if you knew what to do with them. And more importantly, those relationships only worked if Puff allowed them to work. Because if you got too close to somebody, if you started building something on your own, if you started to become more than just security—Puff would shut it down. Not directly. But subtly. He'd stop introducing you to people. He'd stop bringing you to certain meetings. He'd create distance. Because he didn't want you to outgrow your role. He wanted you dependent. He wanted you loyal. He wanted you focused on him. And if you started looking elsewhere, he'd remind you who gave you the opportunity in the first place.

But I didn't see that yet. All I saw was the opportunity. I was traveling the world. I was on private jets. I was in rooms with people I'd only seen on TV. I was at award shows. At movie premieres. At parties that regular people would never get invited to. And I thought I was winning. I thought I was building something. I thought I was on my way. And for a while, I was.

But what I didn't realize was that I was building someone else's empire. Not mine. And that realization wouldn't hit me until years later, when it was almost too late.

CHAPTER 12

THE GLAMOUR AND THE GRIND

2001-2004
Ages 33-36

The first time I got on a private jet, I couldn't believe it was real. I'd flown commercial plenty of times, but this was different. Leather seats that reclined all the way back. A full kitchen. A bathroom bigger than some apartments I'd lived in. No lines. No security checkpoints. No waiting. You pulled up to the private terminal, walked onto the plane, and took off. That's when I realized this is how rich people live. Not comfortable. Not first class. A completely different world.

My first international trip with Puff was to France. We were shooting a commercial for his cologne, Unforgivable, and not in some studio in New York. We were on a yacht in the French Riviera. I'd never seen anything like it. The yacht was massive. Three levels. Helicopters on the deck. Jet skis. Every kind of water toy you could imagine. The food was whatever you wanted, whenever you wanted it. Fresh seafood. Steaks. Pasta. Desserts flown in from Paris. I stood there looking out at the water thinking, how is this my life right now? Two years earlier I was in a federal prison cell. Now I'm in France on a yacht working for one of the biggest names in music. It felt like a dream.

But it wasn't just the glamour. It was watching a young Black man command that level of respect and resources. Puff wasn't just rich. He was powerful. He'd walk into a room and people moved. Executives. Directors. White people with serious money. They listened. Deferred. Waited for his approval. I watched it thinking, this is what success looks like. Not street success. Not hustler success. Real success. Ownership. Control. Calling the shots. And I wanted that. Not for myself yet, but I wanted to understand it. To see how it worked.

After France, the trips kept coming. Ibiza. Turkey. Russia. Africa. Places I never imagined I'd go, places I couldn't pronounce growing up. And I was getting paid to be there. Not a lot, but enough to send money home, stay fresh, feel like I was moving forward. In Ibiza we stayed at one of the biggest villas in the country. Not a hotel. A private estate. Massive. Secluded. It belonged to the same man who owned Cirque du Soleil. Endless rooms. Views of the water. Staff everywhere but invisible. Everything handled before you asked. Puff moved through it like it was normal. For him, it was. For me, a kid from Polo Grounds who grew up dodging roaches and piss-soaked elevators, it felt unreal.

One night in Ibiza, Puff threw a private party at the villa. Truly private. No phones allowed. When you came in, your phone was taken. No pictures. No videos. No posting. What happened there stayed there. Music loud. Bottles everywhere. Puff in full party mode. Pills. Drugs. Whatever was circulating, he was in it. No balance. Full throttle. This wasn't work. This was release. Later, when Instagram came, everything changed. Phones.

Posting. Leaks. Even Puff posting. Privacy became exposure. Confiscating phones turned into a problem because everyone wanted proof. But back then, before all that, it was different. I wasn't thinking about consequences. I was taking it in. The access. The excess. The contrast. It felt like another level. I didn't understand the cost yet.

And it was exhausting. Days ran twenty, twenty-two hours. Start at eight in the morning, finish at six the next morning, then get a text at seven with the next call time. Your body screamed for rest. Your mind was foggy. Feet aching. But you didn't complain. Puff was doing the same hours. And if he could do it, you could do it. That's what you told yourself. But the difference was simple. Puff was building an empire. I was protecting it. Puff made millions. I made seventy-five thousand. Puff built generational wealth. I lived paycheck to paycheck. I didn't see it then. I saw access. Opportunity. Proximity. I thought that was enough.

Russia opened my eyes in a different way. Moscow. St. Petersburg. The architecture. The history. The Kremlin. Red Square. Walking through buildings where wars were planned and empires built. I kept thinking I'm walking through history. It was humbling and exhausting. Because even there, the work never stopped. Meetings before the hotel. Club checks. Extra rooms. Security sweeps. Constant motion. Saying no wasn't an option. No meant replaceable.

Watching Puff with artists really opened my eyes. During Making the Band, I saw him go off on Aubrey O'Day in the studio. Cameras rolling. Crew watching. Calling her fat. Telling her she wasn't serious. Breaking her down publicly. At first I thought it was harsh. Then I told myself it was tough love. That this was how greatness was made. Looking back, I see it clearly. That wasn't tough love. It was control. Breaking someone down so they'd rebuild themselves in your image. Making them small so they'd chase validation. And it worked.

I saw the same pattern everywhere. Warm one day, cold the next. Praise followed by humiliation. Family one moment, employee the next. It kept people off balance. Unsure. Working harder just to stay close. Security guys who'd been around for years disappeared overnight. No goodbye. No explanation. Just gone. That scared me. Because I knew it could be me.

And then there was the real risk. Clubs. Parties. Every night the same words. "Make sure you got that on you." A gun. I'd say yes. Most times I didn't. After two bids, I wasn't risking a gun charge. I lied and prayed nothing popped off. That life is Russian roulette. One mistake sends you back. I tell young people now, weigh the pros and cons. If one con can cost your life or your freedom, walk away. That job could've cost me my freedom. And it did cost me my family.

Still, I convinced myself I was different. That Puff valued me. He'd say things that made me believe it. "You're family." "You move different." "I trust you." I held onto those words when it got hard. They made me feel like I mattered. Like I was more than security.

One day in Miami he pulled me aside. Asked if I saw the jets, the houses, the access. Asked if I knew what it took to get there. "Everything," he said. Time. Relationships. Peace. Everything. He asked if I was willing to give up everything to be great. And I said yes. Because I thought proximity to greatness would make me great too. I didn't realize I was sacrificing for someone else's dream, not mine.

The trips kept coming. The hours got longer. The grind got heavier. I stayed loyal. Kept proving myself. Waiting for the reward. Waiting to become more than security. But in Puff's world, everyone has a role. Mine was protection. Sacrifice. Availability. And in return I got a paycheck, access, and proximity. Not ownership. Not equity. Just closeness.

And I was learning, slowly and painfully, that proximity is not power.

BOND CHECK #4

PROXIMITY IS NOT POWER

Let me tell you something I wish I'd understood twenty years ago. Being close to money doesn't make you rich. Being close to power doesn't make you powerful. Being in the room doesn't mean you have a voice. I learned this the hard way.

THE LESSON I LEARNED TOO LATE

When I started working for Puff, I thought I was winning. I thought, I'm traveling the world. I'm on private jets. I'm in rooms with billionaires. I'm seeing things most people will never see. And all of that was true. But what I didn't realize was that none of it was mine. The jet wasn't mine. The house wasn't mine. The access wasn't mine. I was just borrowing it. Temporarily. As long as I was useful. And the moment I stopped being useful, it would all go away.

Here's what proximity really is. Proximity is being close enough to see wealth but not close enough to build it. Proximity is being in the room but not having a seat at the table. Proximity is working 20-hour days while the person you're working for makes millions and you make $75,000 a year. Proximity is watching someone else build generational wealth while you're living paycheck to paycheck. That's proximity. And I mistook it for opportunity.

THE QUESTION YOU NEED TO ASK

What are you risking for someone who sees you as replaceable? That's the question I should've asked myself every day. But I didn't. Because I was so caught up in the glamour, the access, the feeling of being somebody, that I didn't stop to think about what I was actually building. I was building Puff's empire. Not mine. I was sacrificing my time, my health, my relationships—for his dream. And he knew it. He told me, "You're not gonna make a lot of money working for me. But you're gonna be rich in relationships." And I believed him. But here's the truth: relationships only matter if you can leverage them. And I couldn't. Because every relationship I built while working for Puff was filtered through him. If I got too close to somebody, if I started building something on my own, he'd shut it down. Not directly. But subtly. He'd stop bringing me to certain meetings. He'd create distance. He'd remind me—without saying it—that my job was to work for him, not to build my own thing.

THE CHOICE POINT

The moment I could've chosen differently was when Puff told me, "You're gonna be rich in relationships, not money." I should've heard that as a warning. I should've realized: If I'm not making real money, if I'm not building equity, if I'm not creating something for myself, then what am I doing? But instead, I heard it as motivation. I thought, Okay, I just need to be patient. I just need to keep grinding. Eventually, it'll pay off. But it never did. Because the system wasn't designed for me to win. It was designed for me to work. To sacrifice. To stay loyal. To protect. To serve. And as long as I did that, I had a job. But the moment I stopped, the moment I needed something, the moment I asked for more—I'd be gone.

A WORD FOR THE READER

If you're reading this and you're working for somebody—whether it's in the streets, in the industry, in corporate America, wherever—you need to ask yourself this question: Am I building something, or am I just working? There's a difference. Building means you're creating equity. You're getting ownership. You're putting yourself in a position where, over time, you'll have something that's yours. Working means you're trading time for money. And the moment you stop trading your time, the money stops. I was working. Not building. And I didn't realize it until it was almost too late.

Let me be clear: I'm not saying don't work for somebody. I'm not saying don't take opportunities when they come. I'm saying: know the difference between an opportunity and exploitation. An opportunity is when somebody invests in you. Trains you. Pays you fairly. Gives you equity or ownership. Sets you up to succeed even after you leave. Exploitation is when somebody uses you. Works you to the bone. Pays you just enough to keep you around. And when you're no longer useful, replaces you. I was being exploited. I just didn't see it. Because I was so grateful for the opportunity that I didn't stop to ask: Is this opportunity actually serving me? Or am I just serving someone else?

Here's what nobody tells you about proximity. Proximity feels like success. When you're on a private jet, it feels like you made it. When you're at a party with celebrities, it feels like you're somebody. When you're in the room with billionaires, it feels like you're on their level. But you're not.

You're staff. And the moment you forget that, the moment you start to think you're more than that, reality will remind you real quick.

I remember one time, we were at an event, and I was talking to this girl. She was interested. We were vibing. Everything was cool. And then Puff walked by and said, loud enough for her to hear: "Damn, shorty, you fucking with the help?" And just like that, she lost interest. Because he reminded her—and me—of my place. I wasn't his equal. I wasn't his partner. I wasn't his friend. I was his employee. And no matter how much time I spent with him, no matter how close I got, that would never change.

THE HARD TRUTH

You can't work your way into ownership. Let me say that again. You can't work your way into ownership. I don't care how hard you work. I don't care how loyal you are. I don't care how many hours you put in. If you're not getting equity, if you're not getting ownership, if you're not building something that's yours—you're just working. And when you stop working, you'll have nothing. That's the reality. And I learned it the hard way.

For ten years, I sacrificed everything. My time. My health. My marriage. My relationships with my kids. I missed birthdays. I missed holidays. I missed moments I'll never get back. All because I thought I was building something. But I wasn't. I was just working. And when I finally left—when my body broke down, when I couldn't do it anymore—I had nothing to show for it. No equity. No ownership. No pension. No safety net. Just memories of places I'd been and people I'd met. And memories don't pay bills.

A FINAL WORD

If you're in a situation where you're close to power, close to money, close to success—ask yourself: What am I building for myself? Not what am I building for them. Not what am I building for the company. Not what am I building for the team. What am I building for me? Because at the end of the day, when it's all said and done, you're the only person who's going to take care of you. Not your boss. Not your company. Not the person you're sacrificing for. You. So make sure you're building something that serves you. Make sure you're getting equity, ownership, or at least experience that you can leverage into something bigger. Because proximity is not enough. Proximity is a trap. And I spent twenty years in that trap before I realized it. Don't make the same mistake I did.

CHAPTER 13

THE MANIPULATION GAME

2004-2006
Ages 36-38

There's a game that gets played when you work for powerful people. It's not a game you know you're playing until you're already deep in it. And by the time you realize what's happening, you're so far in that you don't know how to get out. That game is manipulation. And Puff was a master at it.

The manipulation wasn't obvious. It wasn't crude. It was subtle. Strategic. Almost elegant. And that's what made it so effective.

Here's how it worked. Puff would withhold attention, approval, and acknowledgment until you were desperate for it. And then, when you least expected it, he'd give it to you. A compliment. A moment of praise. A "good job." And that small moment of validation would make you forget about all the times he ignored you, talked down to you, or treated you like you didn't exist.

I saw it with everyone. The artists. The assistants. The producers. The security team. It didn't matter who you were or what your role was. If you worked for Puff, you were subject to the game.

With the artists, it was about their careers. He'd sign them. Get them excited. Make them believe they were about to blow up. And then he'd disappear. He wouldn't return calls. Wouldn't show up to studio sessions. Wouldn't promote their music. And they'd be sitting there, confused, wondering what they did wrong. Did I say something? Did I do something? Why isn't he answering? And then, just when they were about to give up, he'd show up. "Yo, my bad. I've been crazy busy. But yo, I got something for you. We about to go crazy with this." And just like that, they'd light up again. The doubt would disappear. The frustration would vanish. And they'd be right back in, working harder than ever, grateful for the attention.

That's manipulation. Not the loud, aggressive kind. But the quiet, strategic kind. The kind that makes you doubt yourself. Makes you think you're the problem. Makes you work harder just to earn back something you should've had all along.

With the assistants, it was about their worth. Puff would make them feel indispensable one day. "Yo, I don't know what I'd do without you. You keep everything running." And they'd feel valued. Important. Needed. But the next day, he'd act like they were invisible. He wouldn't speak to them. Wouldn't acknowledge them. Wouldn't respond to their messages. And they'd spend the whole day wondering what they did wrong. Was it something I said? Did I mess up? Is he mad at me? And then, out of nowhere, he'd call them. "Yo, where you at? I need you." And just like that, they'd drop everything and come running. Because in that moment, they mattered again.

That's the cycle. Withhold. Give. Withhold. Give. Keep people off balance. Keep them guessing. Keep them desperate for your approval. And they'll work twice as hard just to stay in your good graces.

I fell for it too. I'd go days without Puff saying a word to me. I'd be in the car with him, driving him around all day, and he wouldn't acknowledge me once. He'd be on his phone. In meetings. Talking to other people. And I'd just be there. Present but invisible. And I'd start to question myself. Did I do something wrong? Did I mess up on something? Is he upset with me? I'd replay the last few days in my head, trying to figure out what I could've done differently. But I couldn't find anything. Because I hadn't done anything wrong.

That's the trick. The withholding isn't based on your performance. It's based on control. It's about keeping you in a state of uncertainty so that when he does give you attention, you're so grateful that you'll do anything to keep it. And then, just when I was about to lose it, just when I was starting to think maybe I wasn't cut out for this, Puff would say something. "Yo, Bonds. Good work last night. You moved right." That's it. One sentence. But that one sentence would erase days of silence. Days of doubt. Days of feeling invisible. And I'd be right back in. Okay. He sees me. He appreciates me. I'm good.

But I wasn't good. I was being manipulated. And I didn't even realize it.

The manipulation extended to money too. Puff would dangle opportunities in front of you. "Yo, I got something for you. Just hold tight. I'm gonna take care of you." And you'd believe him. Because why wouldn't you? He's Puff Daddy. He's got more money than you can imagine. If he says he's gonna take care of you, he means it. Right?

Wrong. Because "I'm gonna take care of you" was a promise that never came with a timeline. It could be tomorrow. It could be next month. It could be never. But as long as you believed it was coming, you'd keep working. Keep grinding. Keep sacrificing.

I can't tell you how many times Puff told me, "Yo, Bonds. Don't worry. When I get right, you gonna get right." And I believed him. Every time. But "when I get right" never came. Because Puff was already right. He was making millions. But that money wasn't trickling down to me. Sure, I was making $75,000 a year. And that was more than I'd made in the streets. But I was working 20-hour days. I was traveling the world. I was putting my life on the line. And $75,000 wasn't enough for that.

But every time I thought about asking for more, Puff would say something that made me feel guilty for even thinking about it. "Yo, Bonds. You know how many niggas would kill for this opportunity? You know how many people wish they could be where you at?" And he was right. There were a thousand dudes who would've taken my spot in a heartbeat. So I'd shut up. And I'd keep working.

That's manipulation too. Making you feel guilty for wanting more. Making you feel ungrateful for asking for what you deserve. It's a way to keep you in line without ever having to actually take care of you.

But the manipulation that messed me up the most was the way Puff would play with your emotions. One day, he'd treat you like family. "Yo, Bonds. You my brother, man. I love you. You one of the few people I trust." And you'd feel it. That connection. That bond. You'd think, Okay. This is real. This is more than just a job. But the next day, he'd treat you like an employee. "Yo, why you standing there? Go get the car. Go handle this. Go do that." And you'd be confused. Wait. Yesterday I was your brother. Today I'm just the help?

And that inconsistency—that back and forth between "you're family" and "you're just an employee"—it keeps you off balance. Because you never know which version of Puff you're going to get. So you're always trying to prove yourself. Always trying to earn back that "family" status. Always working harder, sacrificing more, just to feel valued again.

I saw him do this with everyone. And the crazy part? It worked every time. Because people want to be valued. They want to be seen. They want to believe they matter. And Puff knew how to exploit that.

One day, we were in the studio, and Puff was working on Making the Band. This was the reality show where he was putting together a music group. And I watched him tear down this girl named Aubrey O'Day. "Yo, you getting fat. You not taking this seriously. You think you can just coast? Nah. You gotta work harder." He said it in front of everybody. Cameras rolling. Crew watching. And Aubrey just stood there, trying not to cry. At first, I thought, Damn. That's harsh. But then I rationalized it. He's pushing her to be better. He's trying to make her great. That's just how the industry works. But looking back now, I see it differently. That wasn't tough love. That was control. That was breaking somebody down so you could build them back up the way you wanted them.

And it worked. Because the next day, Aubrey was working twice as hard. Trying to prove herself. Trying to earn back his approval. And when Puff finally said, "Okay, that's better," she lit up. Like she'd just won the lottery. Because his approval was the prize.

That's the manipulation game. Break them down. Build them up. Break them down. Build them up. Keep them dependent on your validation. And they'll do anything you ask.

I started to notice the pattern with the security team too. There were guys who'd been with Puff for years. Loyal. Solid. Never missed a day. And then one day, they'd be gone. No warning. No explanation. Just gone. And when you'd ask what happened, people would just shrug. "Man, Puff just moves on."

That scared me. Because it meant that no matter how loyal you were, no matter how hard you worked, you were still replaceable. And that realization—that you're always one bad day away from being cut off—it keeps you in line. You don't complain. You don't ask for more. You don't push back. Because you know that if you do, you could be next.

But here's the thing about manipulation. It only works if you don't see it. And I didn't see it. Not for years. I thought Puff was just being strategic. I thought he was just running his business the way successful people run their businesses. I didn't realize I was being played.

And by the time I did realize it, I was in too deep. I'd already sacrificed so much. My time. My health. My relationships with my family. And I thought, If I leave now, it was all for nothing. So I stayed.

That's the final manipulation. Making you believe that you've invested too much to walk away. Making you believe that if you leave, you lose everything. So you stay. Even when you know you should go.

And that's exactly what I did. I stayed. For years. Because I couldn't see a way out.

But what I didn't realize was that every day I stayed, I was losing more of myself. I was becoming somebody who accepted things I never should've accepted. Somebody who normalized behaviors that should've never been normalized. Somebody who put access and money over dignity and self-respect.

And that's what manipulation does. It doesn't just control your actions. It controls your mind. It makes you believe that the cage you're in is actually freedom. That the scraps you're getting are actually a feast. That the manipulation is actually love.

And by the time you realize what's happening, you've already lost so much time, so much energy, so much of yourself that you don't know how to get it back.

That's where I was. Manipulated. Controlled. Trapped. But still believing I was winning.

CHAPTER 14

WHAT I WITNESSED

2006-2008
Ages 38-40

This is the hardest chapter for me to write. Because it's about something I saw. Something I witnessed. Something I didn't stop. And I'll regret that for the rest of my life.

I need to tell you about Cassie.

I first met Cassie in 2006. She was young. Maybe 19 or 20. Beautiful. Talented. And her song "Me & U" was everywhere. She was signed to Bad Boy. She was the next big thing. And she was dating Ryan Leslie. Ryan was a producer. A talented dude. He'd produced her album. Helped build her career. And from what I could see, they were solid. They seemed happy.

But then Puff started paying attention to Cassie. At first, it seemed professional. He was her boss. She was his artist. But then it became something more. And before long, Cassie wasn't with Ryan anymore. She was with Puff.

The way it happened was strategic. Puff didn't just take her. He made sure Ryan couldn't come around anymore. One day, Puff said, "Yo, if Ryan shows up at the office, don't let him in." Just like that. Ryan was cut off. From the studio. From the sessions. From Bad Boy. Not because he did anything wrong. But because Puff had taken his girl, and he didn't want to deal with the awkwardness of seeing him. I remember thinking, Damn. That's cold. But I didn't say anything. Because it wasn't my place. At least that's what I told myself.

At first, Cassie and Puff seemed happy. She'd travel with us. Be at the studio. Be at the parties. And Puff would show her off. "Yo, this is my girl. This is Cassie." And she'd smile. She seemed happy. But over time, things changed.

The first thing I noticed was the arguing. It would start with something small. A comment. A tone. A look. And then it would escalate. "Why you talking to him?" "Why you dressed like that?" "Who told you to do that?" And Cassie would try to explain. Try to defend herself. Try to calm him down. But it never worked. Because Puff wasn't looking for an explanation. He was looking for control.

The arguments got more frequent. And louder. I'd be in the car, sitting in the front seat, and I'd hear them in the back going at it. Or I'd be standing outside a door, and I'd hear yelling from inside. And I'd just stand there. Not knowing what to do. Because my job was to protect Puff from external threats. Not to get involved in his personal life. At least that's what I told myself. But deep down, I knew. I knew what was happening wasn't right.

One day, Cassie came downstairs to smoke with me. We were in Miami. Puff was upstairs. And she came down to the courtyard where I was. And

I saw it. A bruise. Under her eye. She had makeup on, trying to cover it. But I could still see it. I didn't say anything at first. I just looked at her. And she looked at me. And we both knew. But neither of us said anything. She lit her cigarette. I lit mine. And we stood there in silence. I wanted to ask. I wanted to say something. But I didn't know what to say. And part of me thought, Maybe it's not what I think. Maybe she fell. Maybe it was an accident. But I knew. Deep down, I knew.

The second time I saw her with a bruise, I couldn't stay silent. "Yo, Cassie," I said. "You good?" She nodded quickly. "Yeah. I'm good." "You sure?" She looked at me. And for a second, I thought she was going to tell me the truth. But then she just repeated, "I'm good, Bonds." And that was it. I wanted to push. I wanted to ask more questions. But I also knew: if I said too much, she'd go back and tell Puff. And then I'd have a problem. So I let it go. And I hated myself for it.

The incident that I'll never forget happened in Los Angeles. We were at an awards show on Sunset Boulevard. I don't remember which one. But I remember what happened. We were at the event, and Cassie was talking to somebody. I think it was a manager or a producer. Somebody in the industry. And Puff saw her talking to this person. And I saw his face change. That shift from calm to something else. He walked over to her. Fast. And before I could even register what was happening, he grabbed her. Not gently. Hard. And he started yelling at her. Right there. In front of people. "What the fuck you doing? Who is that?" And Cassie tried to explain. "Baby, that's just—" But he wasn't listening.

I moved closer. Not to intervene yet. Just to be ready. And then Puff pushed her. Not hard enough to knock her down. But hard enough to send a message. And then he hit her. Slapped her. Open hand. Across the face. Once. Twice. And people were watching. Not a lot. But enough. I didn't think. I just moved. I stepped between them. Grabbed Puff. Pulled him back. "Yo. We gotta go. Now." And I grabbed Cassie and pushed her toward the exit. "Go. Get to the car." She ran. Crying. Makeup running down her face. And I turned back to Puff. "Come on. Let's go." He was breathing hard. Angry. But he followed me. And we got to the car.

The whole ride back, Cassie was in the back seat, crying. And Puff was still angry. "Yo, that bitch was disrespecting me. You saw that, right, Bonds? She was talking to that nigga like I wasn't even there." I didn't say anything. I just drove. Because I didn't know what to say.

When we got back to the hotel, Puff said, "Yo, Bonds. Take her to the Lennox Hotel. Get her a room. I'll deal with her tomorrow." So I took Cassie to the hotel. The whole drive, she didn't say a word. Just cried quietly. And I didn't know what to say. So I said nothing. When we got to the hotel, I checked her in. Got her a room. Walked her to the door. And before she went inside, she looked at me. "Thank you, Bonds." And I nodded. But I didn't feel like I deserved thanks. Because I didn't stop it. I just moved her out of the way after it already happened.

That night, I sat in my hotel room, and I couldn't sleep. I kept replaying what I saw. What I did. What I didn't do. And I asked myself: What the fuck am I doing? This wasn't security work. This wasn't protecting somebody from a threat. This was being complicit in abuse. And I knew it.

But the next day, everything went back to normal. Puff called Cassie. They talked. She came back. And nobody said anything about what happened. Not me. Not her. Not him. It was like it never happened. Except it did happen. And it kept happening.

Over the next two years, I witnessed more arguments. More fights. More bruises. And every time, I told myself the same thing: It's not my place. It's not my business. But I knew better. I knew I was watching a young woman get abused. And I was doing nothing about it.

I talked to Cassie about it twice. The first time, I said, "Yo, Cassie. You don't have to stay. You know that, right?" She looked at me like I was crazy. "What are you talking about?" "I'm just saying. If you wanted to leave, you could." She shook her head. "I'm good, Bonds." And she walked away.

The second time, I was more direct. "Yo. Why do you stay? Why do you put up with this shit?" And she got defensive. "Put up with what?" "You know what I'm talking about." She stared at me for a long time. And then she said, "He loves me, Bonds. He just... he gets stressed. But he loves me." And I realized: she believed it. She believed that what was happening was love.

Both times I talked to her, she went back and told Puff. And Puff pulled me aside. "Yo, Bonds. Mind your business." That was it. Just those four words. And I knew: if I pushed it again, I'd be gone.

So I stopped. I stopped asking her about it. I stopped talking to her about leaving. And I just watched. And I hated myself for it.

But here's what I didn't understand at the time. I was asking Cassie why she stayed. But I should've been asking myself the same question. Why was I staying? I told myself it was because I needed the job. Because I had a family to support. Because I didn't have other options. But the truth was simpler. I was scared. Scared of losing the income. Scared of losing the access. Scared of going back to nothing. And so I stayed. Just like Cassie.

We were both trapped. She was trapped by fear, manipulation, and what she thought was love. I was trapped by money, loyalty, and proximity to power. But we were both trapped.

And the worst part? I started to normalize it. I started to think, Well, this is just how it is. This is just how powerful people operate. I started to justify it. Rationalize it. Accept it. And that's when I knew I was losing myself.

Because the person I was before—the person who grew up in Polo Grounds, who had sisters, who had a mother—that person would've never stood by and watched a woman get abused. That person would've said something. Done something. But I wasn't that person anymore. I'd become somebody who put money and access over morality. And I didn't know how to get back to who I used to be.

One night, I was sitting with Nick, and I said, "Yo. This shit with Cassie. It's not right." Nick looked at me. "I know." "So why are we just standing here watching it?" He sighed. "Man. What are we gonna do? It's his girl. It's his business." "But we're part of it," I said. "We're here. We're watching it happen. That makes us part of it." Nick didn't say anything. Because he knew I was right. We were complicit.

And the thing that haunted me most was thinking about my own daughters. I had four daughters at that time. And if some dude was putting his hands on one of my daughters, I'd want somebody to step in. To say something. To protect her. But here I was, watching somebody else's daughter get abused. And I was doing nothing.

I tried to reconcile it in my mind. I told myself, Cassie's an adult. She can leave if she wants to. But I knew that wasn't how abuse worked. It's not about logic. It's about control. Manipulation. Fear. And Cassie was trapped in a cycle she couldn't see her way out of. And so was I.

Every time I witnessed something, I'd tell myself, This is the last time. Next time, I'm saying something. Next time, I'm doing something. But I never did. Because every time I got close to speaking up, I'd think about my paycheck. My family. My responsibilities. And I'd stay quiet.

But staying quiet was killing me. Not physically. But mentally. Emotionally. Spiritually. I was compromising everything I believed in just to keep a job. And I didn't know how much longer I could do it.

One day, Cassie and I were outside smoking again. And out of nowhere, she said, "Do you think I'm stupid?" I looked at her. "What?" "For staying. Do you think I'm stupid?" And I didn't know what to say. Because the truth was complicated. I didn't think she was stupid. I thought she was trapped. Just like me. So I said, "Nah. I don't think you're stupid. I just think... I think you deserve better." She nodded slowly. And for a second, I saw something in her eyes. A flicker of clarity. Of truth. But then it was gone. And she went back inside.

That was the last real conversation we had about it. After that, we just existed in the same space. Both of us knowing what was happening. Both of us unable to stop it.

And I started to realize something profound. Being close to power doesn't just corrupt you with money or access. It corrupts you morally. It makes you accept things you'd never accept anywhere else. It makes you complicit in things you'd never be complicit in anywhere else. And it changes you. Slowly. Quietly. Until you don't recognize yourself anymore.

That's what was happening to me. I was becoming somebody I didn't recognize. Somebody who could watch a woman get abused and do nothing. Somebody who could justify it by saying, "It's not my business." Somebody who valued money over morality. And I hated that person. But I didn't know how to stop being him.

Because every day I stayed, I was making a choice. A choice to prioritize my comfort over someone else's safety. A choice to be complicit over being courageous. A choice to keep my job over keeping my integrity. And those choices added up. Day after day. Month after month. Year after year. Until I looked in the mirror and didn't recognize the man staring back at me.

That's what proximity to power cost me. Not just time or health or relationships. It cost me my soul. And by the time I realized it, I'd already paid a price I could never get back.

CHAPTER 15

THE PARTIES AND
THE DRUGS

2006-2009
Ages 38-41

If you've ever wondered what it's like at the top, let me tell you. It's not what you think. It's excess. It's chaos. It's a lifestyle that looks glamorous from the outside but is unsustainable from the inside. And the parties were where you saw it all.

The parties weren't like regular parties. They were productions. Hundreds of people. Sometimes thousands. A-list celebrities. Models. Athletes. Executives. Bottles flowing. Music blasting. Energy through the roof. And drugs. Everywhere.

I need to be clear about something. In all my years working for Puff, I never saw him—or anyone around him—sneak drugs to somebody. I never saw anyone slip something into someone's drink. I never saw anyone drug someone without their knowledge. What I saw was open. Public. Consensual. "Yo, you want one of these?" "Here, take this. It'll keep you up." "We're partying tonight. Pop one of these." And people would take them. Not because they were forced. But because they wanted to be part of the scene. They wanted to fit in. They wanted to keep up. They wanted to be in the inner circle. And if taking a pill was the price of admission, they'd take it. I'm not saying that makes it right. I'm just saying that's how it was. The drugs were part of the culture. Part of the lifestyle. And if you wanted to be in that world, you accepted it.

The parties usually started late. Midnight. 1 AM. Sometimes later. And they'd go until 6 or 7 in the morning. And Puff would be there the whole time. Working the room. Networking. Making moves. Because even at a party, Puff was working. But to keep up with that schedule—to go from a full day of work straight into an all-night party and then start the next day a few hours later—you needed help. And that help came in the form of pills. Uppers. Stimulants. Whatever kept you awake and alert.

At first, I didn't take them. I'd just drink coffee. Red Bull. Whatever. But after a while, coffee wasn't enough. Because the schedule was brutal. 20-hour days. 22-hour days. Sometimes 24 hours straight. And I couldn't afford to be tired. If I was tired, I couldn't do my job. I couldn't protect Puff. I couldn't read the room. I couldn't spot threats. So I started taking pills too. It started with one. Just one, to get through a long night. And it worked. Suddenly, I wasn't tired anymore. I was alert. Focused. Ready. And the next day, when I was exhausted from being up all night, I'd take another one just to function. And before I knew it, I was taking them regularly. Not to get high. But to survive.

That's the thing about that lifestyle. It's not sustainable without help. You can't work 20 hours, party until 6 AM, and then start again at 8 AM without something keeping you going. And everybody knew it. Puff took them. The artists took them. The assistants took them. Security took them. It was just part of the job. And because everyone was doing it, it felt normal. It didn't feel like drug use. It felt like work. Like, This is just what you have to do to keep up. But looking back now, I see it for what it was. It was unsustainable. It was unhealthy. It was destructive. And it was slowly killing all of us.

The parties themselves were excessive. Not just the drugs. Everything. The alcohol. The women. The energy. It was like every party was trying to top the last one. More bottles. More people. More chaos. And there were always young women. Everywhere. Models. Aspiring artists. Instagram girls. Influencers. All of them wanting access. Wanting to be close to the power. Wanting to be seen. And they'd do whatever it took to get in.

I remember one night in Miami, this girl came up to me at the rope. "Yo, can you get me in?" "Nah," I said. "It's invite only." She leaned in closer. "Come on. I'll do whatever you want. Just get me in." And she meant it. That's how desperate people were to be in those rooms. And once they got in, they'd do whatever it took to stay. Take the pills. Drink the bottles. Go along with whatever was happening. Because being in that room meant access. Meant opportunity. Meant maybe their life could change. But what they didn't realize was that they were just part of the show. Just another body in the room. Just another person to make the party look good. And when the party was over, they'd be forgotten.

I saw girls leave those parties looking lost. Like they didn't know where they were or how they got there. And sometimes they'd come up to me the next day and ask, "What happened last night?" And I'd think to myself, You took something you shouldn't have taken. And now you don't remember. But here's the thing. Nobody forced them to take it. They took it because they wanted to fit in. Because they wanted to party. Because they wanted to be part of the scene. And when they couldn't handle it, when they had a reaction they didn't expect, it wasn't Puff's fault. At least that's what I told myself at the time.

But now, looking back, I see it differently. Because even though nobody forced them, the environment created the pressure. The culture. The expectation. The normalization of excess. If you wanted to be in that room, if you wanted to stay in that circle, you had to keep up. And if you couldn't keep up naturally, you took something to help you keep up. And Puff knew that. He created that environment. He benefited from that environment. And he didn't do anything to stop it.

I will say this though. If somebody had a bad reaction, if somebody took too much or mixed the wrong things, Puff would help. "Yo, call an ambulance." "Yo, make sure they're with someone. Make sure they get to a hospital." He wouldn't just leave them. He'd make sure they got help. But the fact that it happened so often that we had a protocol for it? That should've been a red flag.

One night in LA, we were at a house party. Private. Invite only. Maybe 50 people. And this girl passed out on the couch. Just completely out. Unresponsive. And everyone was freaking out. "Yo, what did she take?" "Did anyone see what she took?" "Somebody call 911." Puff came over. Looked at her. And said, "Yo, call the ambulance. Make sure they take her through the back. I don't want cameras." And we did. We got her help. She was fine. She went to the hospital, got checked out, and was okay. But the priority wasn't her health. The priority was making sure it didn't become a story. Making sure there were no cameras. No witnesses. No lawsuit. And that's what I started to notice. Everything was about protecting the brand. Protecting the image. It didn't matter what happened, as long as it didn't get out.

One night we came back to the house and Puff was upset. Agitated. Moving different. Everybody's asking, "What happened? What's going on?" Puff looked at me: "Yo, Bonds. Go get thirty thousand out the safe. Give it to Paul." I'm looking at him like, what? "Thirty thousand? For what?" "Just get it, man." So I went to the safe. Pulled out thirty thousand in cash. Gave it to Paul. Later, Paul told me what happened: Puff had smacked some dude in the club. Over Cassie. The dude wanted thirty thousand to make it go away. To not press charges. To not make it a thing. And that was it. Problem solved. Thirty thousand dollars. Cash. From the safe that we kept for exactly these situations. That's when I realized: This was the system. Puff would do something—hit somebody, disrespect somebody, cause a problem—and we'd pay to make it go away. Thirty thousand here. Fifty thousand there. Whatever it took. And I was the one pulling cash out of the safe to do it. At the time, I thought: Okay, this is just how it is. Rich people problems. We handle it with money and move on. But looking back now, I see what was really happening: He was learning that he could do anything and buy his way out of consequences. Hit somebody? Pay them. Abuse Cassie? Keep her quiet with gifts, trips, promises. Cause a problem? Throw money at it. And it worked. For years, it worked. Until it didn't. Because you can't pay your way out of everything. Some people want you to cash the check that you wrote. They want actual consequences, not just money. But Puff didn't know that. Or didn't believe it. Because for twenty years, money fixed everything. And I was part of that system. Pulling cash out of safes. Helping make problems disappear. Enabling him to avoid accountability. That thirty thousand I handed to Paul that night? That was just one of many times. How many other people got paid off? How many other incidents got buried with cash? I don't know the full number. But I know I was there for enough of them to understand the pattern: Money didn't just buy access and luxury. It bought silence. It bought compliance. It bought the ability to do wrong without consequence. Until the consequences caught up anyway.

The parties became a routine. Every weekend. Sometimes twice a weekend. New York. Miami. LA. Atlanta. Same energy. Same excess. Same chaos. And I was there for all of it. Watching. Protecting. Participating. And I started to realize something. I wasn't just security anymore. I was complicit. I was part of a system that normalized excess. That encouraged reckless behavior. That created an environment where people—especially young women—felt pressured to do things they wouldn't normally do. And I justified it by telling myself, They're adults. They're making their own choices. But were they really? Or were they being manipulated by proximity to power, by the promise of opportunity, by the pressure to fit in?

I started to see the toll it was taking. Not just on me. But on everyone. The artists looked exhausted. Strung out. The assistants looked burnt out. Defeated. The women looked used. Discarded. And I looked in the mirror and saw someone I didn't recognize.

My body was breaking down. I'd gained weight. Lost weight. Gained it back. I wasn't sleeping. Wasn't eating right. My blood pressure was high. My stress was through the roof. And then one day, I went to the doctor, and he told me I had diabetes. "You're pre-diabetic," he said. "But if you keep living like this, it's going to get worse." And I knew what he meant. The late nights. The pills. The stress. The lack of sleep. It was all catching up to me.

But I didn't stop. Because I thought I couldn't stop. I thought if I stopped, I'd lose everything. So I kept going. Taking the pills. Doing the late nights. Surviving on adrenaline and caffeine and whatever else I could find to keep me going. And the parties kept happening. More bottles. More drugs. More excess. And I kept watching. Kept protecting. Kept being complicit.

One night, I was standing in the corner of a party, and I just looked around. Looked at the chaos. The excess. The waste. And I thought to myself, What am I doing here? I saw people passed out on couches. I saw people stumbling around, barely able to stand. I saw young women who looked lost, confused, like they didn't know how they got there or how to leave. And I thought, This isn't success. This is destruction.

But the next morning, we'd be right back at it. Call time at 8 AM. Full day of work. Party that night. And the cycle would repeat. I started to realize that this lifestyle wasn't just unsustainable. It was designed to break you. To make you dependent. To make you willing to do anything just to keep up. And once you were in, once you'd normalized the excess, once you'd accepted the drugs and the chaos and the late nights—you were trapped. Because leaving meant admitting that you couldn't handle it. And nobody wanted to be the person who couldn't handle it.

So we all just kept going. Taking the pills. Working the hours. Surviving the parties. And pretending like it was normal. But it wasn't normal. And deep down, I knew it.

I started to think about my life before this. Before the private jets. Before the parties. Before the excess. And I realized: I was happier then. I didn't have as much money. I didn't have as much access. But I had my health. I had my peace. I had my integrity. And I'd traded all of that for a lifestyle that was slowly killing me.

One night, I was in the bathroom at a party, looking at myself in the mirror. And I saw the toll. The bags under my eyes. The weight I'd gained. The exhaustion written all over my face. And I thought, I can't keep doing this. But I did. For years. Because I didn't know how to stop. And I didn't know what else I'd do if I left.

The parties continued. The drugs continued. The excess continued. And I continued to be part of it. Watching. Protecting. Surviving. But I wasn't living anymore. I was just existing. Going through the motions. Doing what I had to do to get through each day. And hoping that eventually, something would change. But nothing changed. Not until my body forced me to change. Not until I couldn't ignore the toll anymore. Not until I realized that if I didn't walk away, this lifestyle would kill me. And even then, even when I knew I had to leave, it took years before I actually did. Because that's how deep I was in. That's how normalized it had all become. That's how trapped I was.

The parties and the drugs weren't just about having a good time. They were about control. About excess. About creating an environment where people would do things they'd never normally do. And I was part of that environment. For years. And I'll have to live with that for the rest of my life.

BOND CHECK #5

THE PRICE OF NUMBNESS

L et me tell you something about survival. Sometimes, surviving means shutting down parts of yourself. It means accepting things you know are wrong just to get through the day. It means normalizing chaos so you don't lose your mind. But here's what I learned: survival isn't the same as living.

THE LESSON I LEARNED TOO LATE

When I started taking pills to keep up with the work, I told myself it was just temporary. Just until I get used to the schedule. Just until my body adjusts. Just until things slow down. But things never slowed down. And "just this once" became every day. And before I knew it, I couldn't function without them.

That's how addiction starts. Not with a decision to get high. But with a decision to survive. And when you're in an environment where everyone is doing it, where it's normalized, where it's just "part of the job"—it doesn't even feel like you're making a bad choice. It feels like you're doing what you have to do. But here's the truth I didn't see at the time: when you numb yourself to survive, you also numb yourself to living. You stop feeling the joy. The connection. The purpose. You just go through the motions, doing what needs to be done, trying to make it to the next day. And that's not living. That's just existing.

THE QUESTION YOU NEED TO ASK

What are you numbing yourself to? That's the question I should've asked. Because the pills weren't just helping me stay awake. They were helping me avoid feeling the truth: that I was in a toxic environment, that I was watching people get hurt and doing nothing about it, that I was compromising my values for a paycheck, that I was losing myself. And as long as I stayed numb, I didn't have to face any of that. I could just keep going. Keep working. Keep surviving. But surviving isn't enough.

THE CHOICE POINT

The moment I should've walked away was when the doctor told me I had diabetes. That was my body telling me: You can't keep living like this. But I didn't listen. I just added insulin to my routine and kept going. Because I thought I couldn't afford to stop. But the truth is: I couldn't afford not to stop. Every day I stayed, I was paying a price. My health. My relationships. My integrity. My peace. And no amount of money was worth that.

A WORD FOR THE READER

If you're in an environment where you have to numb yourself just to get through the day—whether it's drugs, alcohol, pills, whatever—that's a sign. That's your body, your mind, your soul telling you: This isn't sustainable. And you need to listen. Because if you don't, if you just keep pushing through, keep numbing yourself, keep surviving—eventually, your body will make the choice for you. And by then, it might be too late.

I'm not saying leave your job tomorrow. I'm not saying throw away your career. I'm saying: pay attention to what you're doing to survive. Pay attention to what you're normalizing. Pay attention to the price you're paying. And ask yourself: Is this worth it? Because the lifestyle might look glamorous. The parties might look fun. The access might feel like success. But if you have to numb yourself just to exist in it, it's not success. It's a cage. And the longer you stay, the harder it is to leave.

I stayed for ten years. And I paid for it with my health, my marriage, and almost my life. Don't make the same mistake I did.

THE HARD TRUTH ABOUT EXCESS

Excess isn't freedom. Excess is a trap. It makes you think you're living when you're really just consuming. It makes you think you're successful when you're really just surviving. It makes you think you're in control when the lifestyle is controlling you. I was surrounded by excess for years. Money. Parties. Women. Drugs. Access. And from the outside, it looked like I had it all. But from the inside, I was empty. I was exhausted. Burnt out. Numb. And I didn't even realize it until I was so deep that I couldn't see a way out.

A FINAL WORD

If you take anything from this chapter, take this: your health is your wealth. Not your job. Not your access. Not your proximity to power. Your health. Physical. Mental. Emotional. Spiritual. If you're sacrificing your health for a lifestyle, for a job, for money—you're losing. Even if it looks like you're winning.

I learned this the hard way. I sacrificed my health for a job that didn't care about me. I numbed myself to survive an environment that was slowly killing me. And I normalized behaviors that I knew were wrong just to keep my place in a system that was designed to use me up and throw me away.

Don't do what I did. Don't wait until your body breaks down. Don't wait until you've lost everything that actually matters. Don't wait until you look in the mirror and don't recognize yourself. Pay attention to the signs. Listen to your body. And have the courage to walk away from anything—no matter how glamorous it looks—that requires you to numb yourself just to survive.

PART FOUR: THE UNRAVELING

CHAPTER 16

THE BODY BREAKING DOWN

2010-2012
Ages 42-45

Your body will tell you the truth even when you're lying to yourself. And for years, I'd been lying to myself. Telling myself I was fine. That I could handle it. That I just needed to push through. But my body knew better. And eventually, it forced me to listen.

By 2010, I'd been with Puff for almost ten years. Ten years of 20-hour days. Ten years of international travel. Ten years of late nights and early mornings. Ten years of pills to stay awake. Ten years of fast food at 3 AM. Ten years of no routine, no structure, just constant movement. And my body was starting to fail.

The first sign was the weight. I'd always been solid. Not fat, but not skinny either. Around 200, 210 pounds. But over the years with Puff, I started gaining weight. Not slowly. Rapidly. Within a few years, I was 250 pounds. Then 270. Then 290. And it wasn't because I was eating more.

It was because of the schedule. We'd be up for 20 hours straight, and I wouldn't eat anything substantial. Just grabbing whatever was available when we had a break. Fast food. Hotel room service at 3 AM. Airport food. Whatever. And then when I did eat, I'd eat heavy. Because I was exhausted and hungry and stressed. Pizza at 4 in the morning. Burgers at 2 in the afternoon. Steak and potatoes at midnight. No routine. No structure. No healthy choices. Just survival. And the different time zones made it worse. We'd be in New York one day, Dubai the next, LA the day after that. My body never knew what time it was. Never knew when to sleep. Never knew when to eat. So I just ate whenever I could. Slept whenever I could. And hoped my body would adjust. But it never did.

The second sign was the exhaustion. Not regular tired. Not "I need a good night's sleep" tired. But bone-deep exhaustion. The kind where you wake up more tired than when you went to bed. The kind where even standing up feels like work. The kind where your whole body aches just from existing. I'd be in the car with Puff, driving him somewhere, and I'd feel myself nodding off. My eyes would get heavy. My head would start to drop. And I'd have to slap myself in the face. Bite my tongue. Roll down the window and let the cold air hit me. Whatever it took to stay awake. Because falling asleep on the job wasn't an option. If I fell asleep, I couldn't protect him. And if I couldn't protect him, I was replaceable. So I'd take another pill. Drink another Red Bull. Drink another coffee. Push through. But my body was screaming at me. Stop. Rest. Slow down. And I kept ignoring it. Because I thought I didn't have a choice.

The third sign was the blood pressure. I went to the doctor for a routine checkup in 2011, and he looked at the numbers and said, "Your blood pressure is dangerously high." "How high?" I asked. "High enough that you could have a stroke. High enough that you need to change something.

Now." He prescribed medication. Told me to eat better. Told me to reduce stress. And I nodded and said I would. But I didn't. Because how do you eat better when you're eating on the run? How do you reduce stress when your job is inherently stressful? How do you take care of yourself when taking care of yourself means you can't do your job? So I just took the medication and kept going. And told myself I'd deal with it later.

But then 2011 happened. And everything changed.

I was in Paris with Puff. We were there for fashion week. Meetings. Events. The usual. And I got a phone call. From my ex-wife. "Roderick. It's your son. He got locked up." My heart dropped. "For what?" "Murder." I felt like the ground disappeared from under me. My son. My oldest. In jail. In Africa. For murder. And I was in Paris. Halfway across the world.

I went to Puff immediately. "Yo. I need to go. My son got locked up." And to his credit, Puff didn't hesitate. "Yo. Go. Do what you gotta do. I'll have Paul pick me up tomorrow when we get back to New York." He gave me $12,000 cash right there. "Use this. Get a lawyer. Do whatever you need to do." And I left. Flew from Paris to Africa. Didn't even go home first. Just got on a plane and went.

When I got there, I saw my son. Talked to him. Got him a lawyer. And I realized: this is bad. This isn't something that's going away quickly. This is years. This is a trial. This is serious. And for the first time in a long time, I felt helpless. Because I couldn't fix this. I couldn't throw money at it and make it disappear. I couldn't call somebody. Couldn't pull strings. Couldn't use my connections. This was real life. And it was happening to my son. And there was nothing I could do but be there.

But I couldn't be there. Because I had to go back to work.

I stayed in Africa for a week. Got things set up. Made sure my son had a lawyer. Made sure he knew I wasn't abandoning him. And then I flew back. Back to New York. Back to Puff. Back to the job. And I tried to push it down. Tried to focus on work. Tried to stay present. But I couldn't. Because my son was in jail for murder. In a foreign country. And I was on the other side of the world, driving Puff Daddy to meetings.

The stress was crushing me. I couldn't sleep. Couldn't eat. Couldn't think straight. Every time my phone rang, I thought it was news about my son. Every quiet moment, my mind went to him. To what he was going through. To what I should be doing differently. And my body started breaking down even more.

I started getting chest pains. Sharp pains. Right in the center of my chest. At first, I ignored them. Told myself it was heartburn. Stress. Nothing serious. But they kept happening. In the car. At events. In the middle of the night. And I started to think: What if this is a heart attack? What if I die right here? But I didn't go to the doctor. Because if I went to the doctor, they might tell me I needed to stop working. And if I stopped working, I'd lose everything. So I just kept pushing through. Taking antacids. Taking pain medication. Taking whatever I could to make it through the day.

And then, in 2012, I was in Sardinia with Puff. We were on vacation. Or what passed for vacation when you worked for Puff. Which meant we were still working, just in a beautiful location. And I started feeling off. Really off. I was thirsty all the time. Drinking water constantly but never feeling satisfied. I was going to the bathroom every 20 minutes. Literally every 20 minutes. I was exhausted. More exhausted than usual. And I was losing weight. Rapidly. At first, I thought maybe I had a stomach bug. Or maybe it was something I ate. But it didn't go away.

When we got back to the States, I went to the doctor. And he ran some tests. Blood work. Urine test. All of it. When he came back with the results, his face was serious. "Mr. Rowan. You have diabetes." I stared at him. "What?" "Your blood sugar is dangerously high. You're diabetic. And based on these numbers, you have been for a while." He started explaining what that meant. Insulin. Diet changes. Lifestyle changes. But I wasn't really listening. Because all I could think was: This is it. This is my body telling me it's done.

"How bad is it?" I asked. "Bad enough that if you don't make changes immediately, you're looking at serious complications. Kidney failure. Blindness. Amputation. Heart disease." He paused. "Mr. Rowan. Whatever you're doing right now—the schedule, the stress, the lack of sleep, the eating habits—you can't keep doing it. Your body can't handle it."

And I knew he was right. Because I could feel it. I could feel my body shutting down. Giving up. Saying, I can't do this anymore. But I also knew that if I told Puff I couldn't keep up with the schedule, I'd be done. Because that was the job. The schedule was the job. And if I couldn't do the job, somebody else would.

So I went back to work. Started taking insulin. Started trying to eat better. Started trying to manage it. But I was still working 20-hour days. Still traveling internationally. Still living the same lifestyle that had caused the diabetes in the first place. And it wasn't working.

I'd be in the middle of a day, and I'd feel my blood sugar drop. I'd get shaky. Dizzy. Disoriented. And I'd have to find something sweet. Fast. Before I passed out. Or my blood sugar would spike, and I'd feel like I was going to vomit. My vision would get blurry. My head would pound. And I'd have to excuse myself. Go to the bathroom. Take my insulin. Wait for it to come down. And through all of this, I'm still supposed to be protecting Puff. Still supposed to be alert. Aware. Ready. But I wasn't. I was barely holding it together.

One night, we were in LA, and I felt my blood sugar drop. Hard. I was driving Puff back from an event, and suddenly I couldn't see straight. The road was blurry. My hands were shaking. I was sweating. I pulled over. "Yo. You good?" Puff asked from the back. "Yeah. Just need a second." I grabbed a candy bar from the glove compartment. Ate it as fast as I could. And waited for my blood sugar to come back up. Five minutes later, I was okay. But in that moment, I realized: I could've killed us both. If I'd passed out while driving. If I'd crashed. Not just me. Him too.

And that scared me. Not just because I could've died. But because I realized how far gone I was. How much I'd sacrificed. How much damage I'd done to my body. And for what?

I started having conversations with myself. Late at night. When I couldn't sleep because my blood sugar was off or my chest was hurting or my mind was racing about my son. Is this worth it? Is this job worth your health? Is this money worth your life? And I knew the answer. No.

But I didn't know how to leave. Because this job was all I had. This income. This access. This identity. If I left, who would I be? What would I do?

So I stayed. Even as my body broke down more and more. Even as the doctor kept warning me. Even as I kept having chest pains and blood sugar crashes and moments where I thought, This is it. This is how I die.

But then one day, I had a conversation with the doctor that changed everything.

"Mr. Rowan," he said. "I need to be very clear with you. The lifestyle you're living is not compatible with diabetes. You cannot keep working these hours. You cannot keep traveling like this. You cannot keep living with this level of stress." He looked me in the eye. "If you don't change something, you will die. Maybe not today. Maybe not tomorrow. But soon. And it won't be pretty."

And for the first time, I really heard it. Not as a warning. Not as advice. But as a fact. If you keep doing this, you will die.

And I had to make a choice. Keep the job and risk my life. Or leave the job and risk my livelihood. It wasn't an easy choice. Because even though my body was failing, even though I was exhausted and sick and broken down, I still felt like I needed this job. Like I couldn't afford to leave. But I also knew I couldn't afford to stay.

So I did something I never thought I'd do. I went to Puff and I told him the truth.

"Yo. I need to talk to you about something." "What's up?" he said. "The doctor told me I can't keep up with this schedule anymore. The diabetes. The travel. The late nights. My body can't handle it." He looked at me. And for a second, I saw something in his face. Maybe concern. Maybe annoyance. I couldn't tell. "So what you trying to say?" he asked. "I'm saying I need a different role. Something that's not 24/7. Something that's not security."

He was quiet for a moment. "What you thinking?" "I heard there's an opening at Ciroc. Marketing. I think I could do that. But I'd need you to approve it." He looked at me for a long time. And I could see him calculating. Weighing the options. On one hand, I'd been loyal for ten years.

I'd been there through everything. On the other hand, if I couldn't do the job anymore, what good was I? Finally, he spoke. "Let me think about it."

And I knew what that meant. It meant he was deciding if I was worth keeping in a different capacity. Or if it was easier to just let me go.

A few days later, he came back to me. "Alright. I'll let you go to Ciroc. But I can't pay you what I'm paying you now. You know that, right?" "Yeah. I know." "Alright. We'll figure it out."

And just like that, after ten years as head of security, I was moving to a different role. A role that meant less money. Less access. Less everything. But a role that might let me live.

I didn't know it at the time, but that conversation was the beginning of the end. Not just of my time as security. But of my entire relationship with Puff.

Because once you stop being useful in the way they need you to be useful, everything changes. And I was about to learn that the hard way.

But at least I was still alive. At least my body would have a chance to heal. At least I'd bought myself some time.

Or so I thought.

CHAPTER 17

THE CALL FROM AFRICA

2011
Age 43

There are moments in life that split your world into before and after. Moments that change everything. Moments where you realize that nothing will ever be the same again. For me, that moment came in Paris. In 2011. With a phone call.

We were in Paris for Fashion Week. Puff had meetings. Events. The usual circuit. It was late. Maybe 2 or 3 in the morning Paris time. And I was in my hotel room, finally getting a few hours of sleep. And my phone rang. I looked at the screen. My ex-wife. And immediately, I knew something was wrong. Because she never called me when I was traveling. Never. She knew I was working. She knew I'd call when I could. So if she was calling now, at this hour, it was an emergency.

I answered. "Hello?" And I heard her voice. Shaking. Crying. "Roderick. It's your son." My heart dropped. My oldest son. The one I named after myself. The one who carried my name. "What happened?" I said. "Is he okay? Is he hurt?" "He got locked up." I sat up in bed. "For what?" And then she said the words that changed everything. "Murder."

I couldn't breathe. Murder. My son. My boy. Locked up for murder. "Where?" I asked. "Africa. He's in Africa. They arrested him yesterday." Africa. Not New York. Not New Jersey. Not somewhere I could just drive to. Africa. Thousands of miles away. A different legal system. A different language. A different everything.

"What happened?" I asked. "What are they saying he did?" And she told me what she knew. Which wasn't much. There'd been an altercation. Someone died. My son was involved. That's all she knew.

I got off the phone and just sat there. Staring at the wall. Trying to process what I'd just heard.

My son was 23 years old. He'd grown up without me for most of his life. Because I was in jail. Then I was in the streets. Then I was traveling the world with Puff. I'd missed so much. His childhood. His teenage years. The moments when he needed a father. And now he was in jail. For murder. And I was in Paris.

I didn't sleep the rest of that night. I just sat there, thinking. Thinking about all the choices I'd made. All the time I'd lost. All the moments I'd missed because I was chasing money, chasing status, chasing something that I thought mattered. And now my son was facing life in prison. And I wasn't there.

The next morning, I went straight to Puff. "Yo. I need to go. Family emergency. My son got locked up." Puff looked up from his phone. "For what?" "Murder." And to his credit, Puff didn't hesitate. "Yo. Go.

Do what you gotta do." He reached into his bag and pulled out cash. Counted it out. $12,000. "Here. Use this. Get a lawyer. Handle it. And when you get back, let me know what else you need." I took the money. Thanked him. And I left.

I didn't go back to New York. I went straight to the airport. Got a flight to Africa that same day. And during that entire flight—14 hours—I couldn't stop thinking. I thought about the last time I'd really talked to my son. It had been months. Maybe longer. Not because we were beefing. But because I was always traveling. Always working. Always busy. And when we did talk, it was surface level. "How you doing?" "Good. You?" "Good." That was it.

I didn't know what was going on in his life. Didn't know who he was hanging around. Didn't know what struggles he was facing. Because I wasn't there. And now he was in jail for murder. And I couldn't help but wonder: If I'd been there, would this have happened? If I'd been a father instead of chasing checks, would he have made different choices? If I'd been present, could I have saved him from this?

I didn't have answers. All I had was guilt. Deep, crushing guilt.

When I landed in Africa, I went straight to see him. They took me to the jail. A place I'll never forget. It wasn't like American jails. It was worse. Concrete walls. No real beds. No real toilets. Just filth and darkness and despair. And my son was in there.

When I saw him, my heart broke. He looked smaller than I remembered. Scared. Lost. But when he saw me, he tried to put on a brave face. "What's up, Pops?" "What's up?" I said. "What's up is you're in jail for murder. What happened?"

And he told me. Told me about the altercation. About the guy who died. About how things escalated. And as he talked, I saw it clearly. My son had become me. The same choices I'd made at his age. The same mentality. The same belief that violence was the answer. And I'd passed that down to him. Not intentionally. But through my absence. Through my example. Because even though I wasn't there physically, he knew what I'd done. He knew I'd caught a body. He knew I'd been to jail. He knew I'd lived that life. And in some way, he was trying to follow in my footsteps. Trying to be the man he thought I was.

And I hated myself for it.

"Listen to me," I said. "This is serious. This isn't New York where you might catch a break. This is Africa. You could be here for a long time." He nodded. "I know." "So we're gonna get you a lawyer. We're gonna fight this. But you gotta be smart. You gotta keep your head down. You understand?" "Yeah. I understand."

I spent the next few days setting things up. Found a lawyer. Paid him with the money Puff gave me plus some of my own savings. Made sure my son knew I wasn't abandoning him. That I was going to do everything I could.

But the reality set in quickly. This wasn't going to be quick. This wasn't going to be easy. This was going to be years. A trial. Appeals. All of it. And there was nothing I could do to speed it up.

I stayed for about a week. And then I had to go back. Because I had a job. I had responsibilities. I had bills. And as much as I wanted to stay, as much as I felt like I should stay, I couldn't. So I left my son in that jail.

And I flew back to New York. Back to work. Back to Puff. Back to the life I'd built.

But everything was different now.

When I got back, Puff asked, "How's your son?" "He's hanging in there. Got him a lawyer. Hopefully we can fight it." "Alright. Let me know if you need anything else." And that was it. That was the conversation.

And I went back to work. Back to the 20-hour days. Back to the travel. Back to driving Puff around, standing in corners, being invisible. But my mind wasn't there anymore. My mind was in Africa. With my son. In that jail cell.

Every day, I'd wake up thinking about him. Every night, I'd go to sleep wondering how he was doing. And in between, I'd be doing my job. Protecting Puff. Being present. But I wasn't really present. I was going through the motions.

And the guilt was eating me alive.

Because here I was, traveling the world on private jets, staying in five-star hotels, making money. And my son was in a jail cell in Africa. Facing murder charges. Alone.

How do you reconcile that? How do you enjoy a meal when your son is eating prison food? How do you sleep in a comfortable bed when your son is sleeping on concrete? How do you live your life when your son's life is on hold?

You don't. You just carry the guilt. The shame. The regret. And you keep moving.

Over the next few months, I talked to my son whenever I could. Which wasn't often. Because international calls were expensive. And the time difference made it hard. But when we did talk, I tried to encourage him. "Keep your head up. We're gonna fight this. You're gonna come home." And he'd say, "Yeah, Pops. I know."

But I could hear it in his voice. The doubt. The fear. The realization that his life might be over before it really started.

And I couldn't fix it. I couldn't make it go away. I couldn't use my connections. I couldn't throw money at it and make it disappear. I was powerless.

And that's when I started to question everything.

What was I doing? What was all of this for? I was working for one of the richest men in hip-hop. I was traveling the world. I had access most people would kill for. But my son was in jail. My marriage was falling apart. My health was deteriorating. And for what? A paycheck? Status? The ability to say I worked for Puff Daddy?

It didn't feel worth it anymore.

I started to realize that I'd been chasing the wrong things. I'd been chasing money and access and proximity to power. But I'd neglected the things that actually mattered. My family. My health. My peace.

And now I was paying the price. My son was in jail. Possibly for the rest of his life. And I couldn't help but think: This is my fault.

Not because I committed the crime. But because I wasn't there. Because I chose work over family. Money over presence. Status over fatherhood. And my son paid the price for my choices.

That realization broke something in me.

I started looking at Puff differently. I started looking at the job differently. I started looking at my life differently.

And I started to understand something I should've understood years ago. No amount of money is worth losing your family. No amount of access is worth losing your health. No amount of status is worth losing yourself.

But I was already so deep. Ten years deep. With nothing saved. With no backup plan. With no clear path out. So even though I knew I needed to leave, I didn't know how.

And so I stayed. But something had shifted.

Before the call from Africa, I was all in. I believed in the mission. I believed in the work. I believed that my sacrifice would eventually pay off. But after the call, I couldn't believe that anymore. Because I'd seen the cost. I'd felt the cost. And I knew that if I kept going down this path, I'd lose everything that actually mattered.

My son's case dragged on. Months turned into a year. A year turned into two. And he was still there. In that jail. Waiting for trial.

And I was still here. Working for Puff. Going through the motions. But I wasn't the same person anymore.

The call from Africa had changed me. It had shown me the truth I'd been avoiding for years. That I'd been living the wrong life. Making the wrong choices. Prioritizing the wrong things.

And I couldn't ignore that truth anymore.

So I started making plans. Not to leave immediately. I couldn't afford that. But to create an exit strategy. To find a way out of security. Out of the 24/7 lifestyle. Out of the constant stress.

Because if I didn't get out, I was going to die. Either from the diabetes. Or from the stress. Or from the guilt. But I was going to die.

And I'd already failed my son once by not being there. I wasn't going to fail him again by dying before I could help him get out.

So I started planning. Started looking for opportunities. Started thinking about what else I could do. Started preparing for the conversation I'd eventually have to have with Puff.

Because I knew one thing for certain. I couldn't keep living like this. Something had to change.

And that change started with a phone call from Africa. A phone call that woke me up. A phone call that showed me what I'd been sacrificing. A phone call that forced me to face the truth.

And the truth was simple: I'd been chasing the wrong things. And it was time to find my way back.

CHAPTER 18

THE EXIT STRATEGY

2012
Age 44

After ten years as head of security, I needed an exit strategy. Not because I wanted to leave Bad Boy completely. But because my body was telling me I couldn't keep up with the 24/7 lifestyle anymore. The diabetes. The blood pressure. The stress. The exhaustion. My doctor had made it clear: change something or die. So I had to find a way out.

The opportunity came from an unexpected place. I got a call from someone at Ciroc. One of the executives on the brand team. "Yo, Bonds. We heard you might be looking for something different. We got an opening on the marketing side. You interested?" I was surprised. Not that they called. But that they called without Puff knowing. "How'd you hear that?" I asked. "Word travels. Look, don't tell Puff I called you. But if you're interested, we'd love to have you. You know the brand. You know the culture. You'd be perfect."

I thought about it. Marketing at Ciroc meant regular hours. It meant not being on call 24/7. It meant I could actually have a life. But it also meant less money. Less access. And admitting that I couldn't do security anymore. Still, I knew I didn't have a choice. So I went to Puff.

"Yo. I need to talk to you about something." We were in New York. In his office. Just me and him. "What's up?" he said, not looking up from his phone. "The doctor said I can't keep up with this schedule anymore. The diabetes. The travel. The stress. My body can't handle it." He looked up then. And I saw something in his face. Not concern, exactly. More like calculation. Like he was trying to figure out if I was really sick or if I was just trying to get out.

"So what you saying?" he asked. "I'm saying I need a different role. Something that's not 24/7. I heard there's an opening at Ciroc. Marketing. I think I could do that." He leaned back in his chair. Studied me. "You know I don't usually move people from security to executive roles, right? That's not really how it works." "I know. But I've been with you for ten years. I know the brand. I know the culture. I think I could do it."

He was quiet for a long moment. And in that silence, I realized: he was deciding if I was worth keeping. If the loyalty I'd shown for ten years was worth accommodating my health needs. Or if it was easier to just let me go and find someone new. Finally, he spoke. "Let me think about it."

Those four words hung in the air for three days. Three days where I didn't hear anything. Where I didn't know if I still had a job or not. Three days where I started to realize: this is how little my ten years of loyalty meant.

When he finally called me back, his answer was calculated. "Alright. I'll let you go to Ciroc. But you know I can't pay you what I'm paying you now, right?" "Yeah. I figured." "You're making what, about 80 now?" "Yeah." "I can probably do 60. Maybe 65. But that's it." Sixty-five thousand.

After ten years. After everything I'd done. After all the times I'd put my life on the line. A pay cut.

But I didn't have a choice. So I said yes.

"Alright," Puff said. "We'll make it work. But listen, this is a chance for you. You do good over there, you could move up. You could build some-thing." And there it was again. The promise of "something more." The carrot dangling just out of reach. I should've known better by then. But part of me still believed him. Part of me still thought that if I worked hard enough, if I proved myself again, eventually I'd get what I deserved.

So I took the job. And I moved to Atlanta.

Atlanta was different from New York. The pace was slower. The energy was different. The cost of living was lower. And for the first time in ten years, I had something I hadn't had before: space. Space to breathe. Space to think. Space to figure out who I was outside of being Puff's security.

The job was marketing and brand promotion. My role was to get Ciroc into clubs, into events, into the culture. To make sure bartenders knew about it. To make sure promoters pushed it. To make sure it was the drink of choice in the South. And I was good at it. Because I knew the streets. I knew the clubs. I knew the people. I'd spent ten years moving through those spaces with Puff. I knew how things worked. So I hit the ground running.

But here's what I realized quickly. The Ciroc team already had their structure. They had "Ciroc Boys" in New York and LA. Brand ambas-sadors who promoted the product, threw events, built the culture. But they didn't have anybody doing that in the South.

So I created it. I created "Ciroc Boys South."

I didn't ask permission. I didn't wait for approval. I just did it. I started recruiting people in Atlanta, South Carolina, North Carolina, Louisiana, Philadelphia, Connecticut. People who knew their cities. Who had influence. Who could move product. And I trained them the same way I'd learned. The same way I'd seen Puff operate.

Here's how it worked. I'd book myself to appear at clubs and events throughout the South. But in order to book me, the venue had to buy a certain amount of Ciroc. Cases of it. Not just a few bottles. And I'd show up. Bring the Ciroc Boys. Make it an event. We'd take pictures. Post on social media. Create buzz. And the clubs loved it. Because it drove business.

Within six months, we were moving serious product. Within a year, we'd moved over a million cases in the South alone. And I won the first-ever Ciroc Ambassador of the Year award.

For the first time in a long time, I felt like I was winning. Not because of proximity to someone else's success. But because of my own work. I'd built something. Created something. Made something happen on my own. And it felt good.

When Puff came to Atlanta and saw what I'd built, he was impressed. "Yo, Bonds. I don't know where you got this idea from, but this is fire. Y'all niggas moving work down here." And I felt validated. Like finally, after all these years, he saw me as more than just security. He saw me as somebody who could build. Who could create. Who could execute.

But then something shifted.

We were at Howard University for an award Puff was receiving. While everything looked celebratory on the surface, one of his close friends pulled me to the side. Somebody who he grew up with. Somebody who knew how he really felt. He said, "Yo, Bonds. Puff not really feeling what you're doing."

I was confused. "What you mean?" He said, "He feels like you're moving like you own Ciroc. Like you're acting like it's your brand." I said, "That don't even make sense. I mention Puff all the time. I always give him credit. I always say this is his brand." He nodded and said, "I know. But you built something down here without asking him. And I think he feels like you're getting too big."

And that's when I realized. Puff didn't want me to fail. But he also didn't want me to succeed too much. He wanted me to do well enough to justify keeping me around. But not so well that I didn't need him anymore.

After that conversation, Puff started acting different. He'd be in Atlanta and wouldn't hit me. He'd do events in cities where I had relationships and wouldn't include me. He'd book appearances through other people instead of going through me. And I realized: he was freezing me out. Not completely. But subtly. Enough to remind me of my place. Enough to let me know that no matter what I built, it was still his.

That's when I understood. Even in this new role, even with this "exit strategy," I still wasn't free. I was still dependent on Puff. Still at his mercy. Still subject to his moods and his need for control.

And the promises he'd made? "You do good over there, you could move up. You could build something." Those were just words. Because the moment I started building something real, something independent, he shut it down.

I started to see the pattern clearly now. It was the same pattern I'd seen with artists. With assistants. With everyone who worked for him. He'd give you just enough to keep you hungry. Just enough opportunity to keep you working. Just enough validation to keep you loyal. But never enough to actually be independent. Never enough to actually be free. And I'd fallen for it again.

I thought moving to Ciroc would be different. I thought having a different role would give me more freedom, more autonomy, more control over my life. But it was the same game. Just a different board.

And the salary cut I'd taken? That was intentional too. Because now I was making $65,000. And I had a house. Bills. Responsibilities. So I couldn't afford to leave. I was trapped in a different way. But still trapped.

Over the next few years at Ciroc, I kept building. Kept creating. Kept moving product. But I also kept hitting walls. Anytime I'd get too successful, anytime I'd build too much momentum, something would happen. Puff would make a decision that undercut me. Or Diageo would restructure and my role would change. Or budget cuts would happen and my team would shrink.

And I started to realize: this wasn't an exit strategy. This was just a different cage.

But I didn't know how to get out. Because I'd been in this system for over a decade now. I'd normalized the manipulation. Accepted the control. Justified the treatment. And I didn't know what else I could do. So I stayed. For ten more years, I stayed at Ciroc. Building. Creating. Moving product. Winning awards. Making an impact. But never truly free.

And my relationship with Puff? It got more distant. We'd see each other at company events. At parties. At meetings. But we weren't close anymore. Because once I wasn't with him every day, once I wasn't in his immediate circle, I became less relevant. Out of sight, out of mind.

And I realized something painful. For ten years, I'd thought we had a bond. A relationship. Something real. But it was never real. It was transactional. I was useful when I was protecting him. When I was there 24/7. When I was putting my life on the line. But once I couldn't do that anymore, once my body broke down and I needed something different, the "bond" disappeared.

And that hurt more than I expected. Because I'd sacrificed so much. My health. My family. My marriage. Years of my life. And I'd done it believing that it meant something to him. That I meant something to him. But I didn't. I was just another employee. Another person who worked for him. And when I couldn't work the way he needed me to, I became expendable.

That realization changed everything. It made me see the last decade clearly. All the manipulation. All the control. All the empty promises. I'd been played. For years. And I'd let it happen because I wanted to believe in something bigger than myself. I wanted to believe that proximity to power would eventually give me power. That loyalty would eventually be rewarded. That sacrifice would eventually pay off.

But it doesn't work that way. Not in that world. In that world, you're only as valuable as your current usefulness. And once you stop being useful, you're done.

So my exit strategy didn't really save me. It just gave me a different role in the same system. A system designed to use you up and spit you out. A system where no matter how hard you work, no matter how loyal you are, you'll never really get what you deserve.

And I stayed in that system for another ten years. Not because I wanted to. But because I didn't know how to leave. Because I'd sacrificed too much to walk away with nothing. Because I kept hoping that eventually, things would change. But they never did.

And by the time I finally left—by the time I was finally forced out—I'd lost another decade of my life. Another decade of my health. Another decade of possibilities.

Because an exit strategy is only an exit if you actually leave. And I didn't leave. I just moved to a different room in the same house.

And that house was burning down. I just didn't know it yet.

BOND CHECK #6

THE COST OF STAYING

L et me tell you about the most expensive mistake I ever made. It wasn't going to jail. It wasn't catching a body. It wasn't even getting into the game in the first place. The most expensive mistake I made was staying somewhere I knew I needed to leave.

THE LESSON I LEARNED TOO LATE

When my body broke down, when I got diabetes, when the doctor told me I had to change—I thought I was making a change. I moved from security to marketing. From 24/7 to regular hours. From New York to Atlanta. And I told myself: This is different. This is better. This is my exit. But it wasn't. It was just a different cage. Same system. Same manipulation. Same control. Just dressed up differently.

Here's what I didn't understand at the time: changing positions doesn't mean changing circumstances. I was still working for Puff. Still dependent on his approval. Still subject to his moods and his need for control. I just had a different title. And because I had a different title, because I wasn't in the same role, I convinced myself that things were better. But they weren't better. They were just different. And different isn't the same as free.

THE QUESTION YOU NEED TO ASK

Am I actually leaving, or am I just moving to a different room in the same house? That's the question I should've asked myself when I moved to Ciroc. Because if I'm honest, I knew the answer. I wasn't leaving. I was just repositioning. Hoping that a lateral move would somehow give me what a real exit would've given me. But it didn't. Because you can't escape a system by staying in the system.

I stayed for another ten years at Ciroc. Ten years. And during those ten years, I kept telling myself I was building something. Creating something. Working toward something better. But the truth was simpler and more painful: I was just too scared to leave.

THE CHOICE POINT

The moment I should've walked away was when Puff cut my salary. When he said, "I can't pay you what I was paying you." After ten years of loyalty. After ten years of putting my life on the line. After ten years of sacrifice. He cut my pay. And I accepted it.

I told myself it was because I needed the health insurance. Because I needed a steady paycheck. Because I didn't have other options. But the real reason was fear. Fear of starting over. Fear of being nobody again. Fear of walking away with nothing to show for a decade of work. So I stayed. And I paid for that decision for another ten years.

A WORD FOR THE READER

If you're reading this and you're in a situation where you know you need to leave but you keep finding reasons to stay—listen to me. The cost of staying is always higher than the cost of leaving. Always. I know it doesn't feel that way. I know it feels like leaving means losing everything you've worked for. But staying means losing something more important: time.

You can't get time back. You can get another job. You can make more money. You can rebuild your career. But you can't get back the years you spent in a place that was slowly destroying you. I lost twenty years. Ten years in security. Ten years at Ciroc. Twenty years of my life in a system that used me up and gave me just enough to keep me from leaving. And I can never get those years back.

THE HARD TRUTH ABOUT SUNK COST

There's a term in economics called "sunk cost fallacy." It means continuing to invest in something because you've already invested so much, even when you know it's not working. And that's exactly what I did.

I stayed at Ciroc for ten years because I'd already given ten years to Bad Boy. I told myself: I can't walk away now. Not after everything I've sacrificed. Not after all the time I've put in. But that's backwards thinking. The time I'd already spent? That was gone. I couldn't get it back no matter what I did. The only question that mattered was: What do I do with the time I have left?

And the answer should've been: Leave. Start over. Build something for myself. Find a path where I wasn't dependent on someone who'd proven over and over that he didn't value me. But I didn't. I stayed. Because I was trapped by my own investment.

THE ILLUSION OF PROGRESS

Here's what made it even harder to leave: I was winning at Ciroc. I built Ciroc Boys South. I moved over a million cases. I won Ambassador of the Year. From the outside, it looked like success. And that made it even harder to see the truth: that I was still trapped. Still controlled. Still manipulated.

Because success within a broken system is still a trap. You can be the best worker in a sweatshop. But you're still in a sweatshop. You can be the highest-paid person in a toxic environment. But you're still in a toxic environment. You can win awards and accolades and recognition. But if you're not free, none of it matters. And I wasn't free. I was just successful at being trapped.

WHY IT'S SO HARD TO LEAVE

Let me be real with you about why leaving is so hard. It's not just about money. It's not just about fear. It's about identity.

For twenty years, my identity was tied to Puff. I was "Puff's security guy." I was "Bonds from Bad Boy." I was "the guy who travels with Diddy." That's who I was. And walking away meant giving up that identity. It meant becoming nobody again. And that terrified me.

Because when you've built your entire sense of self around a job, around a person, around a position—losing that feels like losing yourself. Even when that job is killing you. Even when that person doesn't value you.

Even when that position is destroying your health and your family. You hold on. Because letting go feels like dying.

But here's what I learned: you have to let that version of yourself die so a better version can be born. You have to be willing to be nobody for a while so you can become somebody on your own terms. You have to walk away from the identity that's killing you so you can build an identity that gives you life.

THE SIGNS YOU NEED TO LEAVE

Let me give you some signs that it's time to go. Not time to move to a different department. Not time to renegotiate your role. Time to actually leave.

Sign #1: Your health is suffering. If your body is breaking down. If you're taking pills just to function. If you're sick all the time. Leave. No job is worth your health. No paycheck is worth your life.

Sign #2: You're being paid less than you're worth. If you've been there for years and you're still making the same money. Or worse, if you're making less than you used to. Leave. Because that tells you everything you need to know about how much they value you.

Sign #3: You're not growing. If you're doing the same thing year after year. If there's no path forward. If every time you try to build something, it gets shut down. Leave. Because you're not building a career. You're just filling time.

Sign #4: You're compromising your values. If you're witnessing things you know are wrong and doing nothing. If you're participating in things that go against who you are. If you're becoming someone you don't recognize. Leave. Because the money you're making isn't worth losing your soul.

Sign #5: You keep telling yourself "just one more year." If you've been saying "I'll leave next year" for the past five years. Leave now. Because that year will never come. You'll always find a reason to stay one more year. Until suddenly ten years have passed and you're still there.

A FINAL WORD

I know leaving is scary. I know you've invested so much time, so much energy, so much of yourself that walking away feels impossible. I know you're worried about money. About health insurance. About what you'll do next. I know all of that because I felt all of that.

But I'm here to tell you: the cost of staying is always higher than the cost of leaving. I stayed for twenty years. And I paid for it with my health, my marriage, my relationship with my kids, and almost my life. I missed my son's childhood because I was chasing a check. I destroyed my body because I was chasing proximity to power. I lost myself because I was too scared to walk away.

Don't make the same mistake. Don't wait until your body forces you out. Don't wait until you've lost everything that actually matters. Don't wait until twenty years have passed and you look back with nothing but regret.

If you know you need to leave, leave. Not next year. Not when you've saved enough money. Not when you've found something else. Now.

Because every day you stay is a day you'll never get back. And those days add up to years. And those years add up to a life you didn't want to live.

I can't get my twenty years back. But you can save yours.

ACT III: BREAKING THE BONDS

PART FIVE: THE RECKONING

CHAPTER 19

CIROC YEARS AND THE SLOW FADE

2012–2024
Ages 45–56

They say the worst kind of death is the slow one, the kind where you don't even realize you're dying until you're almost gone. That's what the Ciroc years were for me. A slow death of hope. Of expectation. Of belief. And I didn't even see it happening until it was almost over.

When I moved into Ciroc in 2012, I was hopeful. I really believed this was my fresh start, my chance to finally build something for myself. And for the first few years, it felt real. I built Ciroc Boys South from the ground up, recruited brand ambassadors in every major Southern market, trained them, taught them how to move. We threw events, booked appearances, moved product, and we were good at it. By 2013, the South had moved over a million cases, more than any other region, and I won the first-ever Ciroc Ambassador of the Year award.

For the first time in a long time, I felt proud. I felt like I'd built something. Not just protected something. Not just maintained something. I created it. I executed it. I made it successful. But that pride didn't last long. Because as soon as the South started getting real recognition, things shifted. Not loudly. Not directly. Quietly.

As I stated in the last chapter, I later found out—during an award Puff was receiving at Howard University—that he wasn't feeling what I was building. One of his close friends pulled me aside and told me straight up: Puff felt like I was moving like I owned Ciroc, like I was getting too big. I was confused then, and I stayed confused for a long time after that. Everything I did was under the Bad Boy and Ciroc umbrella. I always gave him credit. But perception mattered more than truth.

By the time I really noticed it, the shift had already happened. Puff would come to Atlanta and not hit me. I wouldn't even know he was in town until after he'd left. I'd see it online or hear about it through somebody else. When I asked him about it, he'd keep it light. "Oh man, I was just in and out. Didn't have time." But it wasn't just Atlanta. He started doing events in cities where I had real relationships—Charlotte, Columbia, New Orleans—and I wouldn't be included. I'd see photos on social media, Puff at clubs I'd helped build, with people I'd introduced him to, and I wouldn't get the call.

That's when the money started changing. Bookings I used to get—where promoters would pay me to appear and I'd take a percentage—started drying up. Not because the demand was gone, but because I was being cut out. That's when it really hit me. Even though I'd moved into Ciroc, even though I wasn't security anymore, even though I had a title, I was still under his control. He still decided what opportunities I got. He still decided how far I could go. And the moment I started building something that didn't fully rely on him, the door slowly closed.

Hope doesn't die all at once. It fades.

By 2018, my marriage was already over in every way that mattered, even if it wasn't legally done yet. I was living in Atlanta. She was in South Carolina. We were separated by distance, stress, years of absence, and everything the lifestyle had taken from us. Still married on paper, but the relationship was gone. Life didn't slow down. My son was still in Africa, still fighting his case, still waiting. Legal fees kept piling up. Lawyers. Appeals. Years passing with no resolution. I was drowning.

By 2019, my situation had already changed in a major way. Puff shut down Blue Flame, the company that handled his brand marketing, and when that happened, I was no longer an employee. I was switched to a contract worker. No salary. No benefits. No security. Just a yearly agreement they could choose not to renew. After everything I'd built in the South, after the numbers, the awards, the loyalty, I was now operating year to year. I took it because I didn't feel like I had a choice. I was already deep in the system, and walking away didn't feel possible yet.

In 2020, when the pandemic hit and work dried up, I had no choice but to come back to South Carolina. I moved back into the house, living upstairs while she lived downstairs. Same roof. Different lives. That's when it became clear there was no fixing it. We were just waiting for the inevitable. That same year, I finally pressed Puff about the promise he'd made me over the years. Not because he owed me anything, but because of our history and because of how many times I'd put my life on the line for him.

In 2020, Puff gave me $20,000. At the time, it felt different. It felt real. He told me, "You a hundred percent right. I'm wrong. We gonna get your son home. Whatever we gotta do, we gonna do it." He put his friend Corey—who had just come home after being pardoned from a life sentence—in charge as the liaison. He gave me two other people who managed his money and said, "Whatever Bonds need, give it to him. We getting this moving." For the first time in a long time, I believed him.

But two months later, everything went quiet. No responses. No movement. No updates. When I finally heard back, they told me, "Bonds, we gave you the $20,000. We don't have anything else for you." After that, I couldn't get Puff on the phone again. Just like that, it was over. Back to silence. Back to distance. Back to normal.

That's when I finally understood something I'd been avoiding. Access isn't loyalty. Titles aren't security. Proximity doesn't mean protection. When I was useful, the door stayed open. When I needed something, it stayed shut.

In 2021, I was brought back as a freelancer—not salaried—to help revive Ciroc and DeLeón in the South Carolina market. Sales were down. Numbers were slipping. I went back to work, built relationships again, reworked strategy, and by the end of it, I'd increased Ciroc's numbers in that market by more than thirty percent. It worked.

In 2023, when it was time to renegotiate my contract, the Ciroc manager told me I'd be renewed. Everything seemed lined up. Then Puff sued Diageo, and everything changed overnight. Contracts froze. Communication stopped. Diageo cut ties. In June 2023, I received an email. No call. No conversation. "Due to recent developments, we will not be renewing your contract." That was it. Twenty years. Gone.

I called Puff. "Yo, did you know they were cutting me off?" "Yeah, man. They cutting everybody off. It's fucked up. But don't worry. I'm gonna take care of you." I'd heard that before. Months passed. Nothing.

Then in November, he called. "Yo, Bonds. I might need a favor from you." I thought this was finally it. "What's up?" "I can't talk about it right now. But I might need you. Just stand by." I stood by.

And then my phone started blowing up. Messages. Calls. Texts. "Yo, did you see the lawsuit?" "Your name is in Cassie's lawsuit." I looked it up. And there it was. Cassie's filing. My name mentioned—not as a perpetrator, but as someone who had checked on her. Tried to help. That's when I understood why he'd called. Not to help me. But to see where I stood.

A few days later, he settled the lawsuit. Thirty million dollars. In less than twenty-four hours. And I thought about every time I'd asked him for help. For my son. For my family. For years. He had the money. He always had the money. He just didn't think I was worth it.

By the end of 2023, I had nothing to show for twenty years but memories—and regret. The Ciroc years weren't a new beginning. They were a slow fade. A gradual erosion of hope, value, and self-worth. But the fade wasn't finished yet. Because in 2024, I'd have to make a decision I'd been avoiding my entire life.

Stay silent. Or finally tell the truth.

CHAPTER 20

THE LAWSUIT

November 2023 - March 2024
Age 56

S ome mornings change everything. November 17, 2023, was one of those mornings. I woke up to my phone buzzing. Not just a few notifications. Dozens. Hundreds. Calls. Texts. DMs. Emails. All saying the same thing. "Yo, did you see the lawsuit?" "Bonds, your name is in it." "Yo, call me ASAP." "Bonds, what happened?"

I didn't know what they were talking about. So I opened my phone and started reading. Cassie had filed a lawsuit against Puff. Cassandra Ventura v. Sean Combs. Filed in federal court. November 16, 2023. The allegations were extensive. Sexual assault. Physical abuse. Sex trafficking. Rape. Years of abuse. Years of control. Years of manipulation. And it was all there. In black and white. In legal language. Everything I'd witnessed. Everything I'd suspected. Everything I'd tried not to see.

But what stopped me cold was seeing my name. The lawsuit mentioned me specifically. It said I was one of the only people who ever tried to help her. That I'd checked on her multiple times. Asked if she was okay. That

I'd intervened during violent incidents. That I'd driven her to a hotel after Puff had beaten her in Los Angeles. And it was all true. Every word of it.

I sat there staring at my phone, and I felt sick. Not because I was in the lawsuit. But because reading it made everything real. All those years of telling myself it wasn't my business. All those years of convincing myself that Cassie was an adult who could leave if she wanted to. All those years of justifying my silence by saying I needed the job. None of it mattered now. Because the truth was out. And my name was attached to it.

My phone kept buzzing. Friends. Family. People I hadn't talked to in years. "Yo, Bonds, you okay?" "Man, I didn't know all that was happening." "Bonds, what are you going to do?" I didn't know what I was going to do. I just knew I couldn't ignore this.

Within 24 hours, Puff settled the lawsuit. 24 hours. On November 16, Cassie filed. On November 17, it was settled. $30 million. Thirty million dollars to make it go away. No trial. No discovery. No public testimony. Just money. And a nondisclosure agreement.

And I sat there thinking about all the times I'd asked Puff for help with my son. All the times he said he'd get back to me. All the years my son spent in an African prison while I begged for help. Puff gave Cassie $30 million in less than 24 hours. But he could only give me $20,000. This is the same man that looked me in my eyes on several occasions and said "I could never get $100 million and not take care of my man." That's when I knew for certain: I'd been played for twenty years.

But the lawsuit wasn't over. Even though Puff settled with Cassie, the damage was done. The truth was out there now. And other people started coming forward. In December, another lawsuit was filed. Joi

Dickerson-Neal. Accusing Puff of sexual assault in 1991. Then another one. Liza Gardner. Accusing Puff and singer Aaron Hall of sexual assault in the early 1990s. Then another. An anonymous woman. Jane Doe. Accusing Puff of gang rape when she was 17. One after another. The lawsuits kept coming. And with each one, the picture became clearer. This wasn't just about Cassie. This was a pattern. Decades long. Multiple victims.

From the moment the reporters started reaching out, my heart dropped. This was sometime in 2024. I can't remember the exact day, but I remember the feeling. Confusion. Fear. Shock. Because I had no idea what was going on, or why my name was suddenly coming up.

The first thing I did was lawyer up. I reached out to an attorney immediately. I told him who I was, what the calls were about, and what little information I had. From that day on, I lived my life on guard. Watching everything. Saying very little. Trying to understand what storm I had just been pulled into.

I did speak to Puff one time before he settled with Cassie. He called me and said, "Bonds, I may need you." At the time, I thought he meant business. I figured it was about the liquor he had just come out with, DeLeón. That was my assumption. I had no idea that what he really meant was legal. I had no idea that my name was already in the lawsuit. He said to me, "Bonds if the reporters reach out, let them know that all you saw was regular relationship stuff, nothing crazy." All I could think of was "Here he goes again, trying to control the narrative."

Then the reporters came. They weren't just asking about Puff. They were asking about me. About my movements. About my past. About allegations I had never even heard before. People started making up stories. Wild stories.

One reporter from the New York Post told me that a woman claimed she was in Tokyo while Puff had a performance. She claimed that later on me and her went to the hotel and that she performed oral sex on me, and that Puff walked in. I told the reporter, "Ma'am, when did this supposedly happen?" She said, "In 2000." I said, "If you print that, I will sue you and everyone connected to that article." Because not only have I never been to Tokyo in my life, in 2000 I was incarcerated at FCI Islandwood. I wasn't even home. I told her to do her homework. I told her that if she ran that story, I would own the New York Post.

What hurt the most was how far they went. She didn't just call me. She called my daughter. When I asked how she even got my daughter's phone number, she said, "We get numbers from the library. Sometimes they're right, sometimes they're wrong." That broke me. My daughter had to hear something that disgusting. Something that wasn't true. Something that never happened. And it made me realize how reckless this whole thing had become. People were saying anything. Printing anything. Destroying reputations without caring who they hurt.

The truth is simple. I had nothing to do with anything like that. I would never stand by abuse. I don't condone it. I never have. And I never will.

To this day, reporters still call me. From the U.S. From overseas. From everywhere. And the facts remain the same. I have never been contacted by federal authorities. I have never spoken to investigators. I have never taken the stand. I have never testified for Sean Combs or against Sean Combs.

Everything else is speculation. Rumors. Lies told by people who never bothered to check the truth. And that's the part people don't talk about. How fast a narrative can be created. How easily a person can be pulled into something they had nothing to do with. How quickly silence gets mistaken for guilt. But the truth is the truth. And it hasn't changed.

Even though I never spoke to investigators, there came a point where staying silent no longer felt right. That's why I chose to tell the truth in the Netflix documentary *Sean Combs: The Reckoning*.

By the time the documentary came together in late 2025, the narrative around Puff had already taken on a life of its own. Rumors were everywhere. Speculation was louder than facts. People who were never there were speaking with certainty, while people who had actually been in the environment stayed quiet.

The producers weren't looking for defenders or attackers. They were looking for people who had real proximity and were willing to be honest about what they saw, what they didn't see, and what they could not speak on. Tony Yayo, who knew my character and my history, told 50 he should reach out to me because he trusted that I would tell the truth without embellishment and without an agenda. That mattered to me.

I didn't participate to clear my name. I didn't participate to protect anyone. And I didn't participate to pile on. I participated because truth matters, especially when silence has already done damage.

I understood that being present in an environment doesn't automatically make you complicit, but I also understood how power works. How silence works. How proximity can confuse people into thinking they're safer staying quiet than being honest. I had lived that lesson already. I wasn't interested in repeating it.

So I spoke about what I saw. I spoke about what I experienced. And I was clear about what I was not present for. I didn't speculate. I didn't exaggerate. I didn't fill in gaps that weren't mine to fill. I stayed inside my truth, because anything else would've been dishonest.

By that point in my life, after cancer, after fatherhood, after finally understanding the cost of silence, I knew this much for sure: staying quiet just to avoid discomfort is not integrity. Telling the truth didn't feel easy. But it felt necessary.

And for the first time in a long time, choosing truth over silence felt like choosing the right side of history.

CHAPTER 21

CANCER AND CLARITY

2024
Age 58

They say God has a way of getting your attention. Sometimes it's a whisper. Sometimes it's a shout. And sometimes it's a life-threatening illness.

In early 2024, I started noticing something was off. I was going to the bathroom constantly. Every hour. Sometimes more. And it wasn't like normal. It was urgent. Painful. I'd wake up in the middle of the night three, four times just to pee. At first, I ignored it. Told myself it was just the diabetes. Or stress. Or getting older. But it didn't go away. Then I started noticing other symptoms. Pain in my lower back. Fatigue. More than usual. And blood in my urine. That's when I knew I couldn't ignore it anymore.

I went to the doctor in March 2024. Right in the middle of everything happening with Puff. Right after the federal raids. Right as the walls were closing in on the life I'd known for twenty years. The doctor ran tests. Blood work. PSA test. Digital exam. And when he came back with the results, his face was serious. "Mr. Rowan, your PSA levels are extremely elevated." "What does that mean?" "PSA stands for prostate-specific antigen. Normal levels are between 0 and 4. Yours is 13.9." I stared at him. "What does that mean?" I asked again. "It means we need to do more tests. But it's likely prostate cancer."

Cancer. The word hung in the air like a death sentence. "How bad is it?" "We won't know until we do a biopsy. But based on these numbers, it's significant." I sat there in that doctor's office, and my whole life flashed in front of me. Fifty-eight years old. And I might be dying. Not from a bullet. Not from the streets. Not from any of the dangerous situations I'd survived. But from cancer. From my own body turning against me.

The biopsy confirmed it. Prostate cancer. Stage one. "The good news," the doctor said, "is that we caught it early. Stage one means it hasn't spread beyond the prostate. That means it's treatable." "What are my options?" "Surgery. Radiation. Hormone therapy. Or a combination." He walked me through each option. The risks. The side effects. The success rates. And I had to make a decision about my life.

I chose radiation. Twenty-eight sessions. Five days a week. For just over five weeks. But I also did something else. I went to see an herbalist. Because I'd seen what Western medicine did to people. I'd seen the side effects. The complications. The way it sometimes killed you while trying to save you. And I wanted a holistic approach. I wanted to fight this cancer with everything I had. The herbalist put me on a regimen. Soursop. Black seed oil. Seamoss. Bitters. Teas. Natural remedies that had been used for generations. And I combined that with the radiation. Western medicine and Eastern medicine. Science and nature. I was fighting this thing from every angle.

But the treatment wasn't the hard part. The hard part was sitting with the reality of my mortality. For the first time in my life, I couldn't ignore the fact that I was going to die someday. Not in some abstract, distant future. But potentially soon. And that realization forced me to ask questions I'd been avoiding for decades. What have I done with my life? What do I have to show for fifty-eight years? What will I leave behind?

And the answers were painful. I'd spent twenty years working for a man who didn't value me. I'd sacrificed my health, my marriage, my relationship with my children. I'd been complicit in abuse. I'd stayed silent when I should've spoken up. I'd chased money and access and proximity to power. And what did I have to show for it? A failed marriage. Diabetes. High blood pressure. Cancer. A son in prison. Broken relationships with my daughters. No savings. No career. No security. Just regret. Deep, crushing regret.

And sitting in that radiation chair, five days a week, getting zapped with beams designed to kill the cancer cells in my prostate, I had time to think. Time to reflect. Time to face the truth. The truth was: I'd been slowly killing myself for twenty years. Not with a gun. Not with drugs. But with stress. With sacrifice. With putting everyone else before myself. I'd worked myself sick for a man who gave me $30 million to make a lawsuit go away in 24 hours but couldn't give me $20,000 for my son without making me wait months. I'd stayed silent about abuse because I was scared of losing a job that was already destroying me. I'd normalized behaviors that I knew were wrong because I didn't want to rock the boat.

And my body had kept score. Diabetes. High blood pressure. Now cancer. My body was telling me what I'd been too scared to admit: this lifestyle was killing me. But here's what I realized sitting in that radiation chair. I wasn't dead yet. I still had time. I still had breath. I still had a choice. I could keep living the way I'd been living—surviving, compromising, staying silent. Or I could choose something different.

I could choose to actually live. To speak up. To tell the truth. To prioritize what actually mattered. To be the man I should've been all along. And that's when the clarity came. Cancer didn't just threaten my life. It clarified it. It showed me what mattered and what didn't. It showed me who I wanted to be and who I'd been. It showed me that I'd been wasting my life chasing the wrong things. And I couldn't waste another day.

Because in June 2024, while I was going through radiation, something else happened. My girlfriend gave birth to our daughter. Kennedi. My sixth child. My fourth daughter. I was fifty-eight years old with a newborn baby. Most people would think that's crazy. And maybe it is. But for me, it felt like a sign. A sign that life wasn't over. That I had another chance. That God wasn't done with me yet.

I held Kennedi in my arms, and I made a promise to her. A promise that I'd be a different father than I'd been to my other kids. That I'd be present. That I'd be there. That I wouldn't sacrifice her for a job or money or anything else. And I made a promise to myself. That I'd live long enough to see her grow up. That I'd beat this cancer. That I'd take care of my health. That I'd prioritize my life. Because I couldn't do for my older kids what I should've done. But I could do it for her.

And that meant getting healthy. Physically. Mentally. Emotionally. Spiritually. I stuck with the treatment. Twenty-eight sessions of radiation. Every herb and tea and remedy the herbalist recommended. I changed my diet. Started exercising. Started managing my stress. I did everything the doctors told me to do and everything the herbalist told me to do.

And in August 2024, I went back for my follow-up. They ran the PSA test again. 13.9 when I was diagnosed. The doctor came back with the results. "Mr. Rowan. Your PSA is down to 1.49." I couldn't believe it. "What does that mean?" "It means the treatment worked. We don't see any signs of cancer right now." I sat there and cried. Not just because I was cancer-free. But because I'd been given a second chance. A chance to live differently. To be different. To do better.

The doctor warned me: "This doesn't mean you're cured forever. Prostate cancer can come back. You'll need to get checked every six months. You'll need to maintain your health. You'll need to stay vigilant." "I will," I said. "I promise." And I meant it.

Because cancer had given me something I'd never had before. Clarity. Clarity about what matters: Family. Health. Truth. Integrity. Clarity about what doesn't matter: Money. Status. Proximity to power. Loyalty to people who don't value you. Clarity about who I want to be: A man who speaks truth. Who protects the vulnerable. Who prioritizes what's right over what's comfortable.

For twenty years, I'd been living in survival mode. Just trying to make it through each day. Each week. Each year. Never thinking about the bigger picture. Never asking if this was the life I actually wanted. Just surviving. But cancer taught me: surviving isn't the same as living.

Living means making hard choices. Speaking uncomfortable truths. Walking away from situations that are killing you even when you don't know what comes next. Living means prioritizing your health, your family, your peace over everything else. Living means being the person you want your kids to be proud of. And I hadn't been living. I'd been surviving. But not anymore.

After the cancer diagnosis, after the treatment, after holding Kennedi in my arms and realizing I had another chance—I made a decision. I was going to tell my story. Not to hurt Puff. Not for revenge. Not for money. But because staying silent had almost killed me. And I wasn't going to die with this story inside me. I wasn't going to die having protected abusers and enabled systems of harm. I wasn't going to die without taking responsibility for my choices and trying to help others avoid the same mistakes.

So I started speaking. Started doing interviews. Started being honest about what I'd witnessed, what I'd done, what I'd failed to do. And it was terrifying. Because speaking up meant losing the little bit of access I had left. It meant burning bridges. It meant facing judgment. But it also meant freedom. Freedom from the weight of secrets. Freedom from the burden of complicity. Freedom from living a lie. And that freedom was worth more than anything Puff had ever given me.

The cancer also taught me something else. It taught me that I can't leave the youth alone. Because I have a newborn daughter. And in eighteen years, she's going to be the age Cassie was when she met Puff. She's going to be navigating a world full of powerful men who will try to manipulate her, control her, use her. And I need to make sure the world she grows up in is different from the world I enabled.

That means speaking up. That means teaching young men and women about manipulation, about abuse, about power dynamics. That means using my story—my failures, my complicity, my awakening—to help others avoid the same traps. Because if I can save one person from making the mistakes I made, if I can help one person recognize manipulation before they're trapped in it, if I can give one person the courage to speak up when I stayed silent—then my story matters. Then my pain has purpose.

That's what cancer gave me. Not just another chance at life. But a reason to live. A reason to speak. A reason to teach. A reason to fight for something bigger than myself. And I'm not wasting it.

Every six months, I go back to the doctor. Get my PSA checked. Make sure the cancer hasn't come back. And every time I get good results, I'm reminded: I'm still here for a reason. Not to go back to the life I had. But to build a new one. A life based on truth. On integrity. On protecting the vulnerable instead of the powerful. A life where I can look my daughter in the eye and know I'm being the man she deserves.

Cancer didn't just threaten to take my life. It gave me my life back. Because for the first time in twenty years, I'm not surviving. I'm living. And I'm never going back.

BOND CHECK #7

WHEN YOUR BODY SPEAKS, LISTEN

Let me tell you something that might save your life. Your body is always telling you the truth, even when you're lying to yourself.

THE LESSON I LEARNED ALMOST TOO LATE

For years, my body was screaming at me. The weight gain. The diabetes. The high blood pressure. The exhaustion. The chest pains. Every single one of those was my body saying: Stop. You can't keep living like this. But I didn't listen. I just took pills to manage the symptoms and kept pushing forward.

And then I got cancer. And my body stopped whispering and started shouting: If you don't change, you're going to die.

That's what it took for me to finally listen. Not the diabetes diagnosis. Not the chest pains. Not the doctor's warnings. Cancer.

And I'm one of the lucky ones. I caught it at stage one. I had treatment options. I survived. But not everyone does.

THE QUESTION YOU NEED TO ASK

What is your body trying to tell you?

Are you exhausted all the time? That's not normal. Are you having chest pains? That's not normal. Are you gaining or losing weight rapidly? That's not normal. Are you sick all the time? That's not normal. Are you having panic attacks? That's not normal.

Your body is trying to tell you something. And the question is: Are you listening?

Because I didn't listen for twenty years. I just kept pushing. Kept surviving. Kept telling myself I'd deal with it later. But later almost became never.

THE CHOICE POINT

The moment I should've made a different choice was when I was diagnosed with diabetes in 2012. That was my body's first major warning: Change your life or die. But instead of leaving the toxic situation, I just moved to a different role and kept going. Instead of prioritizing my health, I just added insulin to my routine. Instead of listening to what my body was telling me, I medicated the symptoms and ignored the root cause.

And twelve years later, I got cancer.

That's what happens when you don't listen to your body. It escalates. First it whispers. Then it talks. Then it yells. Then it screams. And if you still don't listen, it stops you completely.

A WORD FOR THE READER

If you're reading this and your body is trying to tell you something—listen. Don't wait until it's cancer. Don't wait until it's a heart attack. Don't wait until it's too late.

Listen when it's exhaustion. Listen when it's stress. Listen when it's high blood pressure. Listen when it's diabetes. Listen before it becomes something you can't come back from.

Because here's the truth: your job doesn't care about your health. Your boss doesn't care about your health. The system doesn't care about your health. They'll work you until you break. And when you break, they'll replace you.

I worked for Puff for twenty years. Sacrificed my health for twenty years. And when my body broke down, when I couldn't do the job anymore, I got a pay cut and eventually got cut off completely. No thank you. No pension. No healthcare after I left. Just an email saying my contract wasn't being renewed.

So don't sacrifice your health for anyone. Not your job. Not your boss. Not your career. Because at the end of the day, you're the only person who's going to take care of you.

THE HARD TRUTH ABOUT STRESS

Stress kills. Not metaphorically. Literally.

It causes heart disease. High blood pressure. Diabetes. Cancer. Strokes. It destroys your immune system. It ages you. It breaks down your body from the inside out.

And I lived in chronic stress for twenty years. Twenty-hour days. No sleep. Constant travel. Always on alert. Always in fight-or-flight mode. And my body kept the score.

That's what stress does. Your body keeps the score. And one day, the bill comes due.

For me, it came due in the form of diabetes and cancer. But it could've been a heart attack. Could've been a stroke. Could've been sudden death. I'm lucky I got warnings. I'm lucky I had chances to change. Not everyone does.

WHAT HEALING ACTUALLY LOOKS LIKE

Healing isn't just about treating symptoms. It's not about taking a pill and going back to the same lifestyle that made you sick.

Healing is about addressing root causes. It's about asking: What in my life is making me sick? And what do I need to change?

For me, the root cause was clear: the lifestyle. The stress. The job. The choices. And true healing meant changing all of that. Not just taking insulin. Not just doing radiation. But leaving the toxic situation. Reducing stress. Prioritizing health. Building a different life.

That's what healing actually looks like. And it's not easy. It's not comfortable. It's not convenient. But it's necessary.

THE GIFT OF A SECOND CHANCE

Cancer gave me a second chance. A chance to live differently. To be different. To build a life worth living instead of just surviving. And I'm not wasting it.

I'm taking care of my health. I'm managing my stress. I'm prioritizing my family. I'm speaking truth. I'm teaching. I'm trying to help others avoid the mistakes I made.

Because I know not everyone gets a second chance. Some people get the diagnosis and it's already too late. Some people ignore the warnings until there are no more warnings.

I was lucky. I got another chance. And I'm making the most of it.

Even after all that, my body still had more to say. On January 23, 2025—my birthday—I had my toe amputated because of complications from diabetes. That didn't happen out of nowhere. That was the bill coming due for years of ignoring the warnings. Cancer gave me clarity. The amputation reminded me that delayed listening still comes with consequences. I'm grateful to still be here, but I don't confuse survival with being untouched. My body remembers everything.

A FINAL WORD

Your body is the only one you get. You can't replace it. You can't upgrade it. You can't trade it in for a new model. You get one body. One life. One chance.

And if you're sacrificing your health for a job, for money, for status, for anything—you're making a mistake that you can't undo.

Because money can't buy health. Status can't reverse disease. And when you're gone, all the sacrifices you made won't matter to anyone but the people who loved you and wished you'd made different choices.

So listen to your body. Listen when it whispers so you don't have to hear it scream. Make changes when they're uncomfortable so you don't have to make them when it's too late. Prioritize your health now so you can actually enjoy the life you're working so hard to build.

Because what's the point of success if you're too sick to enjoy it? What's the point of money if you're too sick to spend it? What's the point of building an empire if you die before you can see it? Your body is always telling you the truth. The question is: Are you listening?

Don't make the same mistake I did. Don't wait until it's cancer. Listen now. And make the changes your body is begging you to make.

Before it's too late.

CHAPTER 22

THE NEW BABY AND THE NEW MISSION

June 2024
Age 58

Kennedi Rowan was born on June 15, 2024. Seven pounds, three ounces. Twenty inches long. Perfect.

I held her in my arms for the first time, and I cried. Not just because she was beautiful. Not just because I was happy. But because I was fifty-eight years old with a newborn baby, and I knew exactly what that meant. It meant I had one more chance to get this right.

I have six children now. My oldest, Roderick—the one who's been locked up in Africa for thirteen years—he's thirty-eight. My second daughter is thirty-seven. Then I have daughters at twenty-eight, twenty-four, and twenty-one. And now Kennedi. And I'm going to be honest with you: I failed most of them. Not because I didn't love them. I've always loved my kids. But because I wasn't there.

I was too busy chasing money. Too busy working for Puff. Too busy traveling the world. Too busy surviving. And by the time I realized what I'd missed, they'd already grown up. I missed birthdays. Missed graduations. Missed games and recitals and parent-teacher conferences. I missed the everyday moments that make up a childhood.

And you can't get those back. You can't undo the damage of absence. You can apologize. You can try to rebuild. You can be better going forward. But you can't give them back the father they needed when they were young. That guilt has eaten at me for years.

But Kennedi—Kennedi is different. Not because I love her more. But because I have a chance to be different. I'm not working for Puff anymore. I'm not traveling the world. I'm not sacrificing my life for someone else's empire. I'm here. Present. Available. Committed. And I'm going to be the father she deserves. The father I should've been to all my kids.

But Kennedi also represents something bigger to me. She represents why this work matters. Because in eighteen years, she's going to be the age Cassie was when she met Puff. She's going to be navigating a world full of powerful men who will try to manipulate her, control her, use her. She's going to face pressure and temptation and situations where she'll have to choose between what's right and what's easy. And I need to make sure she's prepared for that world.

But more than that—I need to make sure the world is different for her than it was for Cassie. That's my mission now. Not just to be a good father to Kennedi. But to create a world where young women like her are safer. Where they're valued. Where they're protected instead of exploited. And that starts with speaking truth.

After Kennedi was born, after I held her and made that promise to be different, I started asking myself a hard question. What kind of man do I want to be for her? Do I want to be the man who stayed silent about abuse because it was convenient? The man who put money over morality? The man who enabled harm because he was too scared to speak up? Or do I want to be the man who tells the truth even when it's hard? The man who stands up for what's right even when it costs him everything? The man who uses his story to help others avoid the mistakes he made?

The answer was obvious. So I made a decision. I was going to dedicate the rest of my life to helping young people avoid the traps I fell into. And that work started immediately.

I started speaking at schools. Community centers. Youth programs. Telling my story. Being honest about my failures. Teaching them what I wish someone had taught me. I talk to them about manipulation. How to recognize it. How to protect yourself from it. How to know when someone is using you. I teach them about the difference between loyalty and complicity. How loyalty to the wrong person can make you compromise everything you believe in. How sometimes the most loyal thing you can do is walk away.

I talk to them about proximity to power. How being close to money and success doesn't make you successful. How you can be in the room and still not have a voice. How you need to build your own empire, not just work for someone else's. And I talk to them about speaking up. About the cost of silence. About complicity. About accountability. About how staying silent to protect yourself ends up destroying you.

The kids listen. Because I'm not preaching to them. I'm not telling them what to do. I'm just telling them my story. Being honest about what happened. Letting them see the consequences of my choices. And they respond to that.

After every talk, kids come up to me. "Yo, Bonds. That really hit me." "Man, I needed to hear that." "I'm going through something similar right now. What should I do?" And I talk to them. I listen to them. I try to help.

Because that's what I wish someone had done for me when I was young. I wish someone had pulled me aside and said: "Yo, Bonds. That life you're chasing? It's not gonna end the way you think." I wish someone had warned me about the cost of certain choices. I wish someone had taught me to value the right things. But nobody did. So I had to learn the hard way. And I'm trying to make sure these kids don't have to learn the same way.

I also started doing work around domestic violence. Because I witnessed it as a kid—my father beating my mother. And I witnessed it as an adult— Puff abusing Cassie. And I stayed silent both times. And that silence is something I have to live with. But I can use that silence to teach others not to make the same mistake.

I speak at domestic violence organizations. I talk to men about accountability. About recognizing abusive behavior. About intervening when you see it. And I talk to women about recognizing the signs. About knowing when to leave. About understanding that love shouldn't hurt.

Because I saw what abuse does. I saw how it traps people. How it breaks them down. How it makes them believe they deserve it or can't escape it. And if I can help one person leave an abusive situation earlier than they would have, if I can help one person recognize manipulation before they're trapped in it—then my story matters. Then my failures have purpose.

That's what Kennedi gave me. Not just a new chance at fatherhood. But a mission. A reason to wake up every day and do better. Because I look at her and I think: What kind of world do I want her to grow up in?

And the answer is: A world where powerful men can't abuse women without consequences. A world where people speak up instead of staying silent. A world where loyalty means being loyal to what's right, not to who's powerful. A world where young people are taught to recognize manipulation before it traps them.

That's the world I want for Kennedi. And I can't just hope for that world. I have to help build it. So I speak. I teach. I share my story. Even when it's uncomfortable. Even when people judge me. Even when I have to face my own failures over and over again.

Because this isn't about me anymore. This is about the next generation. This is about my daughter. And all the daughters out there who deserve better than what the generation before them created.

I think about my older daughters too. The ones I wasn't there for when they were growing up. The ones who grew up watching me choose work over them. Money over them. Puff over them. And I think: What lessons did they learn from watching me? Did they learn that men aren't reliable? That fathers disappear when things get hard? That money and status are more important than family? I hope not. But I'm scared they did.

So part of my mission now is rebuilding those relationships. Showing them through my actions—not just my words—that I'm different now.

That I prioritize them now. That I'm present now. That I'm the father I should've been all along. It's not easy. Because you can't undo twenty years of absence with a few phone calls and apologies. Trust has to be rebuilt slowly. Consistently. Through action.

But I'm committed to it. Because they deserve a father who's present. Who's available. Who shows up. And I'm going to be that father for the rest of my life.

Kennedi changed everything. She didn't just give me a new purpose. She gave me clarity about what actually matters. It's not money. It's not status. It's not proximity to power. It's family. It's integrity. It's truth. It's using your life to make the world better for the people who come after you.

And that's what I'm doing now. Every day, I wake up and I think: What can I do today to be the man Kennedi deserves? What can I do today to help young people avoid the mistakes I made? What can I do today to make the world safer for women like Cassie and my daughters? And then I do that work.

I speak at schools. I talk to young men about respect and accountability. I work with domestic violence organizations. I share my story—the good and the bad—so others can learn from it. I show up for my kids. For my family. For the people who matter.

And it's not glamorous. There are no private jets. No parties with celebrities. No proximity to fame. But it's real. It's honest. It's meaningful. It's the life I should've been living all along.

People sometimes ask me: "Do you regret your time with Puff?" And the answer is complicated. Do I regret the abuse I witnessed and didn't stop?

Yes. Do I regret the time I missed with my kids? Yes. Do I regret sacrificing my health and my marriage? Yes. But do I regret the experience itself? No.

Because without that experience, I wouldn't have the story I have now. I wouldn't have the lessons I can teach. I wouldn't have the perspective I can share. My pain has purpose now. My failures have meaning now. My story can help others now. And that's what matters.

Kennedi will grow up hearing my story. She'll know about my mistakes. My failures. The times I chose wrong. But she'll also see me doing the work to be better. She'll see me speaking truth. Standing up for what's right. Using my voice to help others.

And I hope that teaches her something important. I hope it teaches her that you don't have to be perfect to do good work. That you can mess up and still make things right. That redemption is possible if you're willing to do the work.

And I hope it teaches her to speak up. To stand up for what's right even when it's hard. To value integrity over convenience. To never compromise herself for anyone. Because that's the lesson I had to learn the hard way. And I'm hoping she can learn it the easier way—by watching me.

That's my mission now. Not to be perfect. But to be present. Not to erase my past. But to learn from it and teach others. Not to pretend I have all the answers. But to share what I've learned and help others find their own way.

Kennedi gave me that mission. And I'm going to spend the rest of my life living up to it. Because she deserves a father who shows up. And the world deserves men who speak up. And young people deserve to hear the truth about what happens when you make certain choices.

I can give them that. Not because I'm special. Not because I'm a hero. But because I'm honest. And honesty is what the world needs right now.

So that's what I'm giving. Every day. In every conversation. In every talk. In every interview. The truth.

And I'm teaching my daughter to do the same. Because the world doesn't need more people who stay silent to protect the powerful. The world needs more people who speak up to protect the vulnerable. And that starts with me.

That starts with being the father Kennedi deserves. The man my older kids deserved. The person I should've been all along. And I'm finally—finally—becoming that person.

Not because I got rich. Not because I got famous. Not because I got successful. But because I almost died. And I realized that none of that other stuff matters if you're not living with integrity.

So that's what I'm doing now. Living with integrity. Speaking with honesty. Showing up with consistency. And teaching my daughter—teaching all young people—to do the same.

That's my mission. That's my purpose. That's what the rest of my life is about. And I'm never going back to the man I was.

Because Kennedi deserves better. And so do all the young people out there who are watching, listening, learning. They deserve the truth. And I'm finally—finally—brave enough to give it to them.

CHAPTER 23

TEACHING WHAT I LEARNED

2024–Present
Age 58

The first time I spoke to a group of young people after everything went down, I was nervous. More nervous than I'd been walking into clubs with Puff where I knew people wanted to hurt him. More nervous than I'd been facing federal charges. More nervous than I'd been getting radiation for cancer. Because this was different. This wasn't about survival. This was about impact. And I didn't know if anyone would listen to me.

It was a youth program in Harlem. Kids ages fourteen to eighteen. Mostly boys. Mostly from the streets. Mostly with the same look I had at that age. The look that says: I've seen too much. I know too much. Don't try to lecture me. I walked in, and they were all sitting there with their arms crossed. Skeptical. Defensive. Ready to dismiss whatever I was about to say. And I understood that. Because that's exactly how I would've been at their age.

So I didn't start with a lecture. I didn't start with "let me tell you what you should do." I started with the truth. "My name is Roger Rowan. Most people call me Bonds." "I grew up right here in Harlem. Polo Grounds projects." "And by the time I was your age, I'd already made choices that would define the rest of my life." I saw a few of them lean in. "I caught my first body when I was nineteen years old." "I went to jail. Came home. Went back to jail." "And when I got out the second time, I thought I'd made it because I started working for Puff Daddy." Now they were really listening. "I worked for him for twenty years. Traveled the world. Private jets. Parties with celebrities. Access to everything." "And I thought that was success." "But you know what I have to show for those twenty years?" I paused. "Diabetes. High blood pressure. Cancer. A failed marriage. Time I can never get back with my kids. And a whole lot of regret." The room was silent.

"So I'm not here to tell you what to do. I'm not here to lecture you." "I'm here to tell you what I learned the hard way. And hope that maybe you can learn it the easier way." And for the next hour, I talked. Not at them. With them. I told them about the streets. About the appeal of fast money and respect and feeling like you're somebody. I told them about the cost. About the bodies. About the jail time. About the guilt that never goes away. I told them about working for Puff. About thinking proximity to power was power. I told them about witnessing abuse and staying silent. About sacrificing everything for someone who saw me as disposable. And I told them about what I'm doing now. About choosing to speak truth. About building something real. About being present for my kids.

When I finished, I opened it up for questions. A kid in the back raised his hand. "So you saying we shouldn't try to get money?" "No," I said. "I'm saying there's a difference between getting money and selling your soul for money." "Get your money. Build your empire. Do what you gotta do." "But don't compromise yourself in the process. Don't sacrifice your health, your family, your integrity." "Because once you lose those things, money can't buy them back." Another kid: "But what if that's the only option? What if it's either hustle or starve?" I nodded. Because I knew that feeling. "Listen, I'm not gonna stand here and act like I don't understand. I grew up in the same projects you're growing up in." "I know what it's like when it feels like you got no options." "But here's what I learned: there's always another option. It might not be easy. It might not be fast. But it's there." "And the choices you make at fourteen, fifteen, sixteen—they follow you for the rest of your life." "I'm fifty-eight years old, and I'm still dealing with choices I made when I was your age."

A girl spoke up: "What about when somebody you love is in a bad situation? How do you help them?" I took a breath. Because I knew she was asking about something real. "You speak up," I said. "Even when it's hard. Even when they don't want to hear it." "I watched someone I cared about get abused for years. And I didn't do enough to help." "I told myself it wasn't my business. That she could leave if she wanted to. That it wasn't my place to intervene." "But that was bullshit. That was me protecting myself instead of protecting her." "So if you see someone in a bad situation—speak up. Get them help. Don't let them suffer alone." "And if you're the one in the bad situation—tell someone. Ask for help. Get out." "Because staying in something that's hurting you never gets better on its own." The room was quiet. Then the girl said: "Thank you." And I knew this work mattered.

That was two years ago. Since then, I've spoken at dozens of schools, youth programs, community centers, churches. And every time, I teach the same core lessons. The lessons I wish someone had taught me.

LESSON ONE: WORD IS BOND

Your word is everything. If you say you're going to do something, do it. If you make a promise, keep it. If you commit to something, follow through. That's what "Word is Bond" means. It means Built On No Deception. It means you're someone people can trust. Someone who stands on their word. Because in the streets, your word is all you have. People won't respect your money or your status if they can't trust your word. And that applies to everything. Your relationships. Your business. Your life. If you want people to trust you, you have to be trustworthy. And that starts with keeping your word.

LESSON TWO: LOYALTY TO THE WRONG PERSON WILL DESTROY YOU

I spent twenty years being loyal to someone who didn't value me. And it almost killed me. So I teach young people: loyalty is important. But it has to go both ways. If you're loyal to someone who's using you, abusing you, manipulating you—that's not loyalty. That's slavery. Real loyalty is reciprocal. It's mutual respect. It's caring about each other's well-being. And if the person you're loyal to is asking you to compromise yourself, hurt others, or sacrifice your future—that's not someone who deserves your loyalty. Walk away. I don't care how long you've been with them. I don't care what they've done for you in the past. If they're destroying you, leave.

LESSON THREE: PROXIMITY IS NOT POWER

This is the one that hits hardest for a lot of young people. Because they see people close to power and think that's the goal. But being close to money doesn't make you rich. Being close to success doesn't make you success-ful. Being in the room doesn't give you a voice. I was in the room with Puff for twenty years. I traveled the world. Met celebrities. Had access to everything. But I wasn't building anything for myself. I was building his empire. Not mine. So I tell young people: don't just work for some-one else's dream. Build your own. Get experience. Learn the game. Make connections. But always be building toward something that's yours. Something that can't be taken away when you're no longer useful.

LESSON FOUR: YOUR BODY KEEPS THE SCORE

Young people think they're invincible. I did too. But your body keeps track of everything you put it through. The stress. The lack of sleep. The poor diet. The trauma. And one day, the bill comes due. I got diabetes at forty-four. Cancer at fifty-eight. And both of those were direct results of how I lived for twenty years. So I tell young people: take care of your body now. Don't wait until you're sick to start prioritizing your health. Don't sacrifice sleep and exercise and good food for money or status. Because you can't buy health. You can't reverse disease with money. And if you destroy your body chasing success, you won't be able to enjoy the success when you get it.

LESSON FIVE: SPEAK UP

This is the hardest one. Because speaking up often costs you something. It cost me my relationship with Puff. It cost me access. It cost me the little bit of security I had left. But staying silent cost me more. It cost me my integrity. My peace. My self-respect. So I teach young people: if you see something wrong, say something. If someone is being hurt, intervene. If you're in a situation that goes against your values, speak up or get out. Because silence makes you complicit. And complicity will eat at you for the rest of your life.

These are the core lessons. But the teaching doesn't just happen in formal talks. It happens in barbershops. On street corners. In DMs. In phone calls. A kid will reach out: "Yo, Bonds. I got a situation. What should I do?" And I talk to them. I listen. I help them think through their options. Not because I have all the answers. But because I've lived through enough to know what certain choices lead to.

Sometimes it's about relationships. "Yo, Bonds. My girl keeps going through my phone. She doesn't trust me. What should I do?" And I ask: "Does she have a reason not to trust you?" And if the answer is yes, I tell them: "Then you gotta rebuild that trust through your actions. Words mean nothing without action." And if the answer is no, I tell them: "Then you gotta have a conversation about boundaries. Trust goes both ways."

Sometimes it's about money. "Yo, Bonds. My man wants me to hold something for him. Says he'll pay me." And I tell them: "If you get caught holding someone else's drugs or guns, you're doing the time. Not them." "They'll tell you they got you. They'll promise to take care of you if something happens." "But when you're sitting in jail, they'll be on the street living their life." "So ask yourself: is it worth it?"

Sometimes it's about violence. "Yo, Bonds. Somebody disrespected me. I can't let that slide." And I tell them: "I understand. I felt the same way when I was your age." "But I caught a body over disrespect. And I had to live with that for the rest of my life." "You think you're tough now. You think revenge is the answer." "But ask yourself: what happens after? You kill somebody, then what?" "You go to jail. You lose your freedom. You destroy your future. You hurt everyone who loves you." "Is your ego worth all that?"

Most of them don't like hearing it. But some of them listen. And even if I only reach one out of ten, that's one life potentially saved.

I also work with formerly incarcerated people. People coming home from jail trying to rebuild their lives. Because I've been there. I know how hard it is. You come home and nobody wants to hire you. You come home and everyone expects you to fail. You come home and the same streets that sent you to jail are right there waiting for you. So I help them navigate that. I connect them with resources. Help them find jobs. Talk them through the frustration. And I'm honest with them about what it takes. "Listen, it's gonna be hard. Harder than you think." "You're gonna apply for fifty jobs and get rejected from all of them." "You're gonna want to give up and go back to what you know." "But if you can get through that first year, if you can stay focused and keep pushing, it gets easier." "Not easy. But easier."

And I tell them about my own journey. About how I came home twice and went back to the streets because I didn't know another way. About how I finally found a legal path but ended up in a different kind of trap. "The goal isn't just to stay out of jail," I tell them. "The goal is to build a life worth living." "And that means doing the hard work. Learning new skills. Building real relationships. Creating something that's yours."

I also do work around domestic violence. Speaking to men about accountability. Speaking to women about recognizing the signs. Because I witnessed my father beat my mother when I was young. And I witnessed Puff beat Cassie when I was an adult. And both times, I didn't do enough. So now I'm trying to make sure others don't make the same mistake. I speak at DV organizations. Men's groups. Survivor support groups. And I'm honest about my own complicity. "I saw abuse happening, and I didn't stop it,"

I tell them. "I told myself it wasn't my business. That she could leave if she wanted to." "But that was me protecting myself. Not her." "And I have to live with that."

I teach men to recognize abusive behavior in themselves. The controlling questions. The isolation. The verbal attacks. The physical violence. "If you're checking her phone constantly, that's abuse." "If you're telling her who she can and can't talk to, that's abuse." "If you're making her feel like she's crazy for questioning you, that's abuse." "And if you're putting your hands on her, that's not just abuse—that's assault." And I teach them that getting help is strength, not weakness. "If you grew up seeing violence, you learned that's how conflicts get resolved." "But you can unlearn that. You can do better." "It takes work. It takes therapy. It takes commitment." "But you can change if you want to."

And I teach women to trust their instincts. "If something feels wrong, it probably is." "If he's isolating you from your friends and family, that's a red flag." "If he's making you feel like you're the problem, that's a red flag." "If he's hurting you and then apologizing and promising to change, that's the cycle of abuse." "And you deserve better." "I don't care how much you love him. I don't care how much he apologizes." "If he's hurting you, you need to leave." "And I know that's easier said than done. I know there are financial reasons, emotional reasons, fear." "But there are resources. There are people who can help. And you deserve to be safe."

The work isn't always easy. Sometimes I get pushback. "Who are you to talk? You didn't do anything to help Cassie." "You were part of the problem. Why should we listen to you?" "You're just trying to make money off your story." And they're not wrong. I was part of the problem. I didn't do enough. I stayed silent too long. But that's exactly why my story matters. Because I can speak from experience about what complicity looks like.

About how easy it is to convince yourself you're not responsible. About how you can normalize things that are clearly wrong. And I can speak from experience about what it takes to change. To face yourself. To take responsibility. To do better.

I'm not claiming to be a hero. I'm not claiming to have all the answers. I'm just claiming to be honest. And that honesty resonates with people. Especially young people who are tired of being preached at by people who've never lived what they're living. They respect that I've been there. That I've made the mistakes I'm warning them about. That I'm not speaking from theory but from lived experience. And that credibility—that authenticity—opens doors. I can reach people that social workers can't reach. I can get through to kids that teachers can't get through to. Because they see me and think: "This dude gets it. He's been where I am." And that makes them listen.

One of the most powerful moments I had was with a seventeen-year-old kid named Marcus. He came up to me after a talk, and he was angry. "Yo, you're telling us not to hustle. But what else we supposed to do?" "My mom's got three jobs and we still can't pay rent." "My little sister needs clothes for school." "You think I'm gonna get a minimum wage job and watch my family struggle?" I understood his anger. Because I'd felt it too. "You're right," I said. "A minimum wage job ain't gonna cut it. I'm not gonna stand here and act like it will." He seemed surprised that I agreed with him.

"But let me ask you something," I said. "What happens when you get caught?" "I won't." "That's what I thought too. And I did." "And when you're sitting in jail, who's taking care of your mom? Your sister?" "You think you're helping them now. But if you go away, you're leaving them worse off than before." He was quiet. "So here's what I'm saying: I'm not telling you not to hustle. I'm telling you to be smart about it." "If you're gonna be in the streets, have an exit plan. Know when you're getting out." "Save your money. Don't blow it on chains and sneakers. Stack it." "And use that money to build something legitimate. Start a business. Invest in yourself." "Don't let the streets be your only option forever." He nodded slowly. "And in the meantime, protect yourself. Don't trust everyone. Don't move sloppy." "Because the same people you're running with will tell on you when they get jammed up." "Trust me. I learned that the hard way too."

A few months later, Marcus reached out to me. He'd gotten a job at a barbershop. Was learning to cut hair. Said he was still making moves on the side but was working on his exit plan. I don't know if he'll make it out. I hope he does. But at least now he's thinking strategically instead of just reacting.

That's all I can do. Plant seeds. Share wisdom. Hope it takes root. Because I can't save everyone. I couldn't even save myself for a long time. But I can tell the truth. I can share what I've learned. I can be present and available and honest. And for some people, that'll be enough to make a difference.

That's what teaching looks like for me. Not standing in front of a classroom lecturing about theories. But being in the trenches, having real conversations, meeting people where they are. And slowly, one conversation at a time, trying to help people avoid the mistakes I made.

Because that's my purpose now. Not to be perfect. Not to pretend I have it all figured out. But to be honest about what I've lived through and hope that honesty helps someone else.

That's all any of us can do. Share what we know. Learn from our mistakes. Do better going forward. And teach the next generation to do the same.

BOND CHECK #8

REDEFINING STRENGTH

For most of my life, I had the wrong definition of strength. I thought strength meant never showing weakness. Never crying. Never admitting you're scared. Never asking for help. I thought strength meant taking whatever came your way without flinching. Getting shot at and not running. Getting disrespected and retaliating. Going to jail and not breaking. I thought strength meant loyalty no matter what. Standing by your people even when they're wrong. Never telling. Never cooperating. Taking your charge like a man. That's what I was taught. That's what the streets taught me. That's what my father modeled. That's what hip-hop glorified. And that definition of strength almost killed me.

THE LIE I BELIEVED

The lie I believed for fifty-eight years was that real men don't show emotion. Real men don't cry. Real men don't admit when they're struggling. Real men don't ask for help. Real men just handle it. So I handled everything. I handled watching my father beat my mother by staying quiet. I handled getting shot at by shooting back. I handled stress by pushing it down and taking pills to keep going. I handled abuse by telling myself it wasn't my business. I handled betrayal by staying loyal anyway. And you know what all that "handling" got me? Diabetes. High blood pressure. Cancer. A failed marriage. Broken relationships with my kids. And twenty years of my life given to someone who saw me as disposable. That's what the old definition of strength cost me.

WHAT REAL STRENGTH ACTUALLY LOOKS LIKE

It took cancer to teach me what real strength actually looks like. Real strength is admitting when you're wrong. It's saying "I made a mistake" and taking responsibility for it. It's facing the consequences of your choices instead of blaming everyone else. Real strength is asking for help. It's admitting you can't do everything alone. It's being vulnerable enough to say "I'm struggling" or "I need support." Real strength is walking away. From toxic situations. From abusive relationships. From people who don't value you. Even when everyone calls you soft or a quitter. Even when you've invested years. Even when you don't know what comes next. Real strength is speaking up. Even when it costs you something. Even when people call you a snitch or a traitor. Even when it means standing alone. Real strength is changing. It's admitting that the way you've been living isn't working. It's being willing to unlearn toxic behaviors and learn healthier ones. It's doing the hard work of becoming a better person. Real strength is being present for your family. It's showing up. Being available. Being emotionally vulnerable with the people you love. It's prioritizing them over money, status, ego. That's real strength. And it's a lot harder than the fake strength I was performing for fifty years.

THE CHOICE POINT

The moment I should've redefined strength was when I first saw Puff hit Cassie. That was my choice point. The old definition of strength said: mind your business. Stay loyal. Don't get involved. The real definition of strength would've said: speak up. Intervene. Protect the vulnerable. But I chose the old definition. I chose the comfortable path. The path that didn't risk my job or my relationship with Puff. I chose fake strength. And Cassie paid the price. That's what the old definition of strength does. It protects the powerful and abandons the vulnerable. It values loyalty to people over loyalty to what's right. It confuses silence with strength when silence is actually cowardice.

STRENGTH FOR YOUNG MEN

This Bond Check is especially for the young men reading this. Because you're being fed the same lies I was fed. Society tells you that real men don't cry. That showing emotion is weakness. That vulnerability is something to be ashamed of. That asking for help means you're soft. And if you believe those lies, they will destroy you just like they almost destroyed me. So let me tell you the truth: It takes more strength to cry than to hold it in. Crying doesn't mean you're weak. It means you're human. It means you're processing pain instead of stuffing it down where it'll eventually destroy you. I didn't cry for years. I thought I was being strong. But really, I was just building up trauma that came out in other ways—anger, violence, stress, disease. When I finally let myself cry—after my cancer diagnosis, after holding Kennedi, after facing what I'd done—that's when I started healing. That's when I actually became strong.

It takes more strength to admit you're struggling than to pretend you're fine. The strongest men I know are the ones who can say "I'm not okay" and ask for help. The weak ones are the ones who suffer in silence until they break—until they hurt themselves or someone else. If you're struggling with depression, anxiety, trauma, addiction—talk to someone. Get help. See a therapist. That's not weakness. That's strength.

It takes more strength to walk away from a fight than to engage. The streets taught me that if someone disrespects you, you have to retaliate. That walking away makes you look soft. That you have to prove you're tough. But here's the truth: anyone can throw a punch. It takes no skill, no intelligence, no real strength to be violent. What takes real strength is walking away when every part of you wants to retaliate. What takes real strength is being secure enough in yourself that you don't need to prove anything to anyone. I caught a body over disrespect. And I had to live with that for the rest of my life. If I could go back, I would walk away. I would let him talk. I would let him feel like he won. Because that five minutes of ego protection cost me years of my life and a man his life. That's not strength. That's stupidity.

It takes more strength to leave a toxic relationship than to stay. Whether it's a romantic relationship, a friendship, a job, or a mentor—if it's toxic, leave. I stayed with Puff for twenty years because I thought loyalty meant staying no matter what. But loyalty to someone who's destroying you isn't strength. It's self-destruction. Real strength is recognizing when something isn't good for you and having the courage to walk away. Even when you've invested years. Even when you don't know what's next. Even when people call you disloyal. Your life is more important than someone else's opinion of you.

It takes more strength to be a present father than to be a provider who's never home. A lot of men think being a good father means making money for their family. And providing financially is important. But your kids don't just need your money. They need your time. Your attention. Your presence. I provided financially for my kids. But I wasn't there. And you know what? They would've rather had a father who was present than a father who sent checks from another country. Real strength is being there. Showing up to the games and recitals. Being available when they need to talk. Being emotionally present even when it's uncomfortable. That's harder than working 20-hour days. And it's more important.

It takes more strength to speak up about abuse than to stay silent. The code of the streets says you don't tell. You don't cooperate. You mind your business. And in some contexts, that makes sense. You don't cooperate with police to save yourself. But when it comes to abuse—of women, of children, of anyone vulnerable—silence isn't strength. Silence is complicity. Real strength is speaking up. Intervening. Protecting those who can't protect themselves. Even when it costs you. Even when people call you a snitch. Even when you lose your job or your friends. Because protecting the vulnerable is more important than protecting the powerful.

THE MYTH OF THE STRONG, SILENT TYPE

We glorify the strong, silent type in movies and music. The man who never talks about his feelings. Who handles everything alone. Who never asks for help. But in real life, that man is dying inside. He's stressed. He's lonely. He's carrying trauma he can't process. And one day, he breaks. He hurts himself or someone else. He has a heart attack or a mental breakdown. Because humans aren't built to carry everything alone. We need connection. We need support. We need to talk about what we're going through. And admitting that doesn't make you weak. It makes you smart. It makes you self-aware. It makes you actually strong.

STRENGTH FOR SURVIVORS

If you've survived abuse—whether as a child or an adult—let me tell you something. You are already strong. You survived. You're still here. That takes incredible strength. But now you have a choice. You can carry that trauma silently, pretending you're fine, pushing through until it breaks you. Or you can do the harder thing: get help. Process it. Heal from it. Healing takes more strength than surviving. Admitting you need therapy takes strength. Talking about what happened to you takes strength. Breaking the cycle so you don't pass that trauma to the next generation— that takes enormous strength.

I grew up watching my father abuse my mother. And for years, I normalized abuse because that's what I saw. It wasn't until I faced that trauma, talked about it, processed it, that I could break the cycle. And now I'm teaching my kids different. I'm showing them what healthy relationships look like. That's the hard work of healing. And it takes real strength.

REDEFINING MASCULINE STRENGTH

The old definition of masculine strength is killing us. Literally. Men die younger than women. We have higher rates of suicide. Higher rates of violence. Higher rates of substance abuse. And a lot of that is because we're taught to suffer in silence. We're taught that asking for help is weakness. We're taught to handle everything alone. And it's killing us. So we need to redefine what masculine strength looks like.

Masculine strength is: protecting the vulnerable, not the powerful. Being emotionally available, not emotionally distant. Admitting mistakes, not pretending to be perfect. Asking for help, not suffering alone. Walking away from violence, not engaging in it. Being present for your family, not just providing financially. Speaking truth, not staying silent to protect your comfort. Building people up, not tearing them down. Taking responsibility, not blaming others. Changing and growing, not staying stuck in toxic patterns. That's what real masculine strength looks like. And the world needs more men who embody that.

A WORD FOR WOMEN

This Bond Check is mainly for men, but I want to say something to women too. If the men in your life are operating under the old definition of strength—if they won't talk about their feelings, won't ask for help, won't admit when they're struggling—understand that they were taught that. Society taught them that. And it's hurting them. You can't force them to change. But you can create space for them to be vulnerable if they choose to. You can tell them it's okay to not be okay. You can encourage them to get help. You can model healthy emotional expression. But also: don't sacrifice your own wellbeing trying to fix them. If they're hurting you in their refusal to get help, you have to protect yourself. You can support them, but you can't save them. Only they can do that work.

MY COMMITMENT

I'm committed to teaching young men a different definition of strength. Not the toxic masculinity I was taught. But real strength. Healthy masculinity. Emotional intelligence. Because I don't want another generation of men to make the mistakes I made. I don't want them to sacrifice their health, their families, their integrity because they think that's what strength looks like.

Real strength is: being honest about your struggles. Getting help when you need it. Walking away from toxic situations. Speaking up about what's wrong. Being present for the people you love. Changing when you realize you're wrong. Protecting the vulnerable. Living with integrity. That's the strength I'm teaching my sons and daughters. That's the strength I'm modeling for the young people I work with. That's the strength that actually builds communities and families and lives worth living. Not the fake strength that looks tough but destroys everything it touches. But real strength that looks like vulnerability and courage and growth.

THE QUESTION FOR YOU

What definition of strength are you operating under? Are you suffering in silence because you think asking for help is weakness? Are you staying in toxic situations because you think walking away is cowardice? Are you holding in emotions because you think showing feelings is soft? Are you protecting the powerful because you think loyalty means silence? If so, I'm telling you: that's not strength. That's fear disguised as strength.

Real strength is doing the hard thing. Admitting you're struggling and getting help. Leaving the situation that's destroying you. Being vulnerable with people you love. Speaking up even when it costs you. That's the strength that will actually improve your life. That's the strength that will break generational cycles. That's the strength that will make you the person your kids can be proud of.

I wish I'd learned this thirty years ago. I wish someone had told me that vulnerability is strength, not weakness. I wish I'd known that walking away is sometimes the strongest thing you can do. I wish I'd understood that loyalty to what's right is more important than loyalty to people. But I know it now. And I'm teaching it to anyone who will listen. Because the world doesn't need more men who think strength means never showing weakness. The world needs more men who understand that real strength is being brave enough to be human. That's the kind of strength that changes lives. That's the kind of strength that heals families. That's the kind of strength that breaks cycles. And that's the kind of strength I'm committed to embodying for the rest of my life.

PART SIX: WORD IS BOND

CHAPTER 24

WHAT I KNOW NOW

Present Day
Age 58

If I could go back and talk to my younger self—to that kid in Polo Grounds projects at fourteen years old, standing on the corner deciding which path to take—I'd tell him everything I know now. But that's not how life works. You don't get to go back. You only get to go forward. So instead, I'm writing this down. For my kids. For the young people I work with. For anyone who might be standing where I was, trying to decide which path to take. This is what I know now that I wish I'd known then.

ABOUT THE STREETS

I know now that the streets don't love you back. When I was young, I thought the streets were family. I thought loyalty in the streets meant something. I thought if I held it down, if I stayed solid, if I proved myself—the streets would take care of me. But the streets don't take care of anybody. The streets will use you up and spit you out. The streets will take your youth, your freedom, your life—and keep moving like you never existed. I know now that every dude I looked up to in the streets—the ones who had the cars and the jewelry and the respect—most of them are dead or in jail. The ones who aren't dead or in jail are broken. Traumatized. Living with regret. There's no happy ending in the streets. There's just different variations of loss. I know now that catching a body doesn't make you a man. It makes you a killer. And you have to live with that for the rest of your life. At nineteen, I thought taking someone's life made me respected. Made me tough. Made me somebody. But now, at fifty-eight, I know it just made me a kid who took another person's future because I didn't know how to handle conflict any other way. And that's not something to be proud of. That's something to carry with regret. I know now that the respect you get in the streets is temporary and conditional. As soon as you go to jail, as soon as you leave the neighborhood, as soon as you're not useful anymore—that respect disappears. But the respect you build through integrity? Through being a good father, a good man, someone who helps others? That respect lasts. That respect matters. That respect you can actually be proud of.

ABOUT LOYALTY

I know now that loyalty without wisdom is dangerous. For years, I prided myself on being loyal. No matter what. No matter who. Loyal to my crew. Loyal to Puff. Loyal to people who didn't deserve it. But I know now that blind loyalty is just another form of stupidity. Real loyalty has boundaries. Real loyalty doesn't ask you to compromise yourself. Real loyalty is reciprocal. If someone is asking you to be loyal to them while they destroy you, disrespect you, or use you—that's not loyalty. That's manipulation. I was loyal to Puff for twenty years. And he discarded me the moment I couldn't do the job the way he needed. That taught me: loyalty to the wrong person will cost you everything. But it also taught me what real loyalty looks like. Real loyalty is the people who showed up for me when

I had nothing to offer them. The friends who checked on me during cancer. The family who forgave me for being absent. The young people who trust me enough to share their struggles. That's real loyalty. And it's mutual. It's earned. It's reciprocal. I know now that you have to be loyal to your values before you're loyal to people. Because people will disappoint you. People will change. People will use you. But if you're loyal to your values—to integrity, to truth, to protecting the vulnerable—you'll never lose yourself. And losing yourself is worse than losing anyone else.

ABOUT POWER AND SUCCESS

I know now that proximity to power is not power. This is the lesson I wish I'd learned earlier than I did. I spent twenty years close to one of the most powerful men in hip-hop. I traveled the world. Met celebrities. Had access to everything. And I thought that made me powerful. I thought that made me successful. But I know now: I was just the help. Being in the room doesn't mean you have a seat at the table. Being close to money doesn't make you rich. Being around success doesn't make you successful. I was a tool. A useful tool, but still a tool. And when I stopped being useful, I was discarded. That's what proximity to power is. It's conditional. It's temporary. It's based on what you can do for them, not on who you are. Real power is building something that's yours. Something that can't be taken away when you're no longer useful to someone else. I know now that success isn't about how much money you make. It's about how much of yourself you keep in the process. I made decent money working for Puff. Not great money, but decent money. But I lost myself in the process. I lost my health. My marriage. My relationship with my kids. My integrity. My peace. So was I successful? No. I was surviving. But I wasn't winning. Real success is building a life you're proud of. A life where you can look in the mirror and respect the person looking back. A life where your kids are proud to call you Dad. A life where you sleep well at night because you're living with integrity. That's success. Everything else is just money. I know now that there's a difference between making money and building wealth. I made money for twenty years. But I didn't build wealth. Because wealth isn't just about the money you earn. It's about what you keep. What you invest. What you build that lasts. I spent everything I made. On bills. On keeping up appearances. On surviving. But I didn't invest in myself. I didn't build anything that could outlast the job. And when the job ended, I had nothing. That's making money. Not building wealth. Real wealth is: Owning something. Having equity. Having investments. Having skills that are marketable outside of one person or one company. Having relationships that open doors. Having a reputation for integrity that makes people want to work with you. I didn't have any of that when I left. I had memories and regrets. So now, everything I do is about building real wealth. Not just making money. I'm investing in relationships. I'm building my reputation as someone who tells truth. I'm developing skills in speaking and teaching. I'm building something that's mine. Something that can't be taken away. That's what I wish I'd done from the beginning.

ABOUT FAMILY

I know now that no career is worth sacrificing your family. This is the lesson that hurts the most. I chose work over my family for twenty years. I told myself I was doing it for them. That I was providing for them. That the sacrifice would be worth it. But I know now: they didn't need my money as much as they needed me. They needed a father who showed up. Who was present at birthdays and graduations. Who knew their friends and their dreams and their struggles. Who was available when they needed to talk. They got a father who sent money from another country.

Who called when he had time. Who showed up tired and distracted when he was home. And I can't get those years back. I missed my oldest son's entire childhood. And he ended up following in my footsteps—making the same mistakes I made because I wasn't there to guide him differently. I missed my daughters growing up. And now they're adults with their own trauma from having an absent father. No amount of money is worth that. No job is worth that. No success is worth that. I know now that being a good father isn't about how much you provide. It's about how present you are. Your kids don't care about the private jets you got on for work. They don't care about the celebrities you met. They don't care about the parties you went to. They care about whether you were at their soccer game. Whether you helped them with their homework. Whether you were there when they needed you. And I wasn't. That's my biggest regret. More than the streets. More than working for Puff. More than staying silent about abuse. My biggest regret is not being the father my kids deserved. But I know now that you can't change the past. You can only change how you show up going forward. So that's what I'm doing with Kennedi. I'm showing up. I'm present. I'm available. I'm being the father I should've been all along. And I'm working on rebuilding relationships with my older kids. Not by making excuses. Not by explaining why I wasn't there. But by showing them through consistent action that I'm different now. That I prioritize them now. That I'm here now. It's not easy. Trust has to be rebuilt slowly. But I'm committed to it for the rest of my life.

ABOUT HEALTH

I know now that your body keeps the score. Everything I put my body through—the stress, the lack of sleep, the poor diet, the pills, the trauma— my body kept track of it all. And one day, the bill came due. Diabetes at forty-four. Cancer at fifty-eight. Both direct results of how I lived for twenty years. I know now that you can't outrun poor health choices. You can't out-earn them. You can't ignore them. Eventually, your body will force you to pay attention. And if you're lucky, like I was, you'll get a warning. A chance to change before it's too late. But not everyone gets that chance. I know now that taking care of your health is not optional. It's essential. You can't enjoy success if you're too sick to enjoy it. You can't take care of your family if you can't take care of yourself. You can't change the world if you're dead. So taking care of your health has to be a priority. Not something you do when you have time. Not something you'll get to eventually. Now. Today. Every day. I know now that mental health is just as important as physical health. For years, I ignored my mental health. I pushed down trauma. I didn't process grief. I suffered through depression without acknowledging it. I thought dealing with mental health was weakness. But I know now: ignoring mental health is what's actually weak. Getting therapy. Processing trauma. Working through depression and anxiety. That takes real strength. And it's necessary if you want to actually heal and not just survive. I'm in therapy now. Working through everything I've been through. Everything I've done. Everything I've carried. And it's hard. But it's necessary. Because I don't want to pass my trauma to the next generation. I want to break the cycle. And that requires doing the hard work of healing.

ABOUT SPEAKING UP

I know now that silence is never neutral. When you see something wrong and you stay silent, you're not staying neutral. You're choosing a side. You're choosing the side of the abuser. The side of the powerful. The side of the system. I stayed silent when I saw Puff abuse Cassie. I told myself it wasn't my business. That she could leave if she wanted to. That it wasn't my place to intervene. But I know now: that was cowardice dressed up as professionalism. I should've spoken up. I should've done more. I should've prioritized her safety over my job. And my silence made me complicit in her abuse. That's something I have to live with for the rest of my life. But I know now that the only way to make up for past silence is present truth-telling. I can't go back and save Cassie from what she went through. But I can speak up now. I can tell the truth about what I saw. I can take responsibility for my complicity. And I can teach others not to make the same mistake. I know now that speaking up will cost you something. But staying silent will cost you more. Speaking up cost me my relationship with Puff. It cost me access. It cost me whatever security I had left. But staying silent cost me my integrity. My self-respect. My peace. And I'd rather lose a job than lose myself. I know now that there's power in telling your truth. For years, I carried secrets. I protected abusers. I stayed silent about what I witnessed. And that weight was crushing me. But when I started speaking up—when I started telling the truth about what I saw and what I did and what I should've done differently—I felt lighter. Not because I'm absolved. Not because I'm forgiven. Not because everything is okay. But because I'm finally being honest. And honesty, even painful honesty, is freeing.

ABOUT REDEMPTION

I know now that redemption is possible. But it's not automatic. You don't get redeemed just because you feel bad about what you did. You don't get redeemed just because you apologize. You don't get redeemed just because time has passed. Redemption requires action. It requires taking full responsibility for what you did wrong. It requires making amends where possible. It requires changing your behavior and doing better going forward. It requires using your story to help others avoid the same mistakes. That's what I'm trying to do now. Not just apologize for my past. But actively work to make things better. I can't undo the abuse I witnessed and didn't stop. But I can speak up about domestic violence now. I can teach young men about healthy masculinity. I can help survivors know they're not alone. I can't get back the years I missed with my kids. But I can be present now. I can rebuild trust through consistent action. I can be the father Kennedi deserves. I can't un-enable the system I was part of. But I can expose it now. I can tell the truth about how it works. I can help others recognize manipulation before they're trapped in it. That's redemption. Not perfection. But action. I know now that you can't redeem yourself by hiding your mistakes. Only by owning them and doing better. Some people want me to be quiet about what I saw and what I did. They want me to protect Puff's legacy. Or protect my own reputation. But I know now: the only way to actually redeem myself is to tell the truth. All of it. The good and the bad. What I saw and what I did and what I should've done differently. That's what accountability looks like. And accountability is the first step toward redemption.

ABOUT LEGACY

I know now that legacy isn't about what you accomplish. It's about who you help. For years, I thought legacy was about being somebody. About making money. About being close to power. About having respect. But I know now: none of that matters if you didn't help people along the way. The money I made is gone. The access I had is gone. The respect I got from proximity is gone. But the young person I helped avoid the streets? That matters. The woman I helped leave an abusive relationship? That matters. The kid I mentored who's now doing better than I did? That matters. That's legacy. Not what you accomplished. But who you helped. I know now that the best way to honor the people you failed is to make sure others don't get failed the same way. I failed Cassie. I failed my kids. I failed myself. But I can make sure other Cassies get helped by people who speak up instead of staying silent. I can make sure other kids have fathers who are present instead of absent. I can make sure other people recognize manipulation before they waste twenty years. That doesn't erase my failures. But it gives them purpose. I know now that your legacy is what you do after you mess up, not whether you mess up. Everyone makes mistakes. Everyone has regrets. Everyone falls short sometimes. The question is: what do you do after? Do you hide? Make excuses? Blame others? Refuse to change? Or do you own it? Take responsibility? Do the work to be better? Use your story to help others? That's what determines your legacy. And I'm choosing the second path. I'm owning my mistakes. I'm taking responsibility. I'm doing the work. I'm using my story. Because that's the only way to turn pain into purpose.

ABOUT PEACE

I know now that peace doesn't come from success. It comes from integrity. I thought peace would come when I made enough money. When I had enough status. When I proved myself. But I had all those things at various points. And I never had peace. Because peace doesn't come from external validation. It comes from internal alignment. Peace comes when who you are in public matches who you are in private. When you're living according to your values. When you can look in the mirror and respect the person looking back. When you're not carrying secrets that eat at you. That's peace. And I have more peace now at fifty-eight with less money and less status than I had at thirty-eight with more of both. Because I'm living with integrity now. I'm telling the truth. I'm being the person I want to be. And that's worth more than anything Puff ever gave me. I know now that you can't buy peace. You have to build it through how you live. Every choice you make either builds peace or erodes it. Choosing integrity over convenience? Builds peace. Choosing truth over comfort? Builds peace. Choosing to help over choosing to profit? Builds peace. Choosing presence over absence? Builds peace. But the opposite choices erode peace. And I spent twenty years making choices that eroded my peace. So even though I had success, I never had peace. Now I'm making different choices. Harder choices. Choices that don't always benefit me. But choices that I can be proud of. And I'm sleeping better than I have in twenty years.

WHAT I KNOW FOR CERTAIN

After fifty-eight years of life—of mistakes and lessons and pain and growth—here's what I know for certain: Your choices matter. Every single one. They compound over time and become your life. Proximity to power is not power. Build your own instead of working for someone else's. Your body keeps the score. Take care of it before it forces you to. Silence is complicity. Speak up even when it costs you. Loyalty without wisdom is dangerous. Be loyal to your values before you're loyal to people. Family is everything. No career is worth sacrificing them. Redemption is possible. But it requires action, not just regret. Your legacy is who you help. Not what you accomplish. Peace comes from integrity. Not from success. You can't change the past. But you can change how you show up going forward. And that's what I'm doing. Showing up differently. Speaking truth. Teaching lessons. Building peace. Being present for my kids. Helping young people. Taking care of my health. Living with integrity. Not perfectly. But honestly. Not because I've figured it all out. But because I'm willing to keep learning. Not because I'm better than anyone. But because I'm trying to be better than I was. That's all any of us can do. Learn from our mistakes. Take responsibility for our choices. Do better going forward. And use our stories to help others avoid the same traps. That's what I know now. And I wish I'd known it sooner. But since I didn't, I'm making sure others do. Because the lessons I learned the hard way don't have to be learned the hard way by everyone. They can learn from my mistakes. From my story. From my pain. And maybe—just maybe—that will make all of it worth something.

CHAPTER 25

BUILT ON NO DECEPTION

Present Day
Age 58

There's a saying that's been with me my whole life. Word is bond. In the streets, it means your word is your currency. Your reputation. Your honor. If you say you're going to do something, you do it. If you make a promise, you keep it. If you give your word, it's as binding as any contract. Word is bond.

But I've come to understand that phrase has a deeper meaning. A meaning I lived in opposition to for most of my life. Word is bond means: Built On No Deception. B-O-N-D. Built. On. No. Deception. It means living without lies. Without pretense. Without manipulation. It means being honest about who you are and what you've done. It means speaking truth even when it's uncomfortable. It means building relationships, careers, and legacies on truth—not on deception.

For fifty-six years, I didn't live that way. I deceived myself about what I was doing in the streets. Told myself I was just trying to survive. That I had no choice. That this was just how it was in the hood. But I had choices. I just made the wrong ones. I deceived myself about working for Puff. Told myself I was building something. That the sacrifice would pay off. That loyalty would be rewarded. But I was building his empire, not mine. And loyalty was one-directional. I deceived myself about the abuse I witnessed. Told myself it wasn't my business. That she could leave if she wanted to. That speaking up would cost me too much. But it was my business. Because when you witness harm and do nothing, you're part of the harm. I lived a life built on deception. Deception of others. But mostly deception of myself. And that deception almost killed me.

THE TRUTH I WAS AVOIDING

The truth I spent years avoiding was simple: I was complicit. Complicit in abuse. Complicit in a system that used people up and spit them out. Complicit in my own destruction. I told myself I was just doing my job. Just surviving. Just being loyal. But those were lies I told myself to avoid facing the truth. The truth was: I saw wrong and did nothing. I witnessed abuse and protected the abuser. I sacrificed my health and family for someone who saw me as disposable. I stayed silent when I should've spoken up. And I did all of it because speaking up, walking away, doing the right thing—it would've cost me. It would've cost me my job. My income. My access. My identity. So I stayed. And I stayed silent. And that silence was a form of deception. Not just deception of others. But self-deception. Deceiving myself into believing I was doing the right thing when I knew I wasn't.

THE MOMENT EVERYTHING CHANGED

The moment everything changed was when I was diagnosed with cancer. Sitting in that doctor's office, hearing the word "cancer," facing my own mortality—that's when the deception became impossible to maintain. Because when you think you might die, all the lies you tell yourself fall away. All the rationalizations. All the justifications. All the excuses. And you're left with the raw truth. The truth was: I'd wasted twenty years of my life. I'd sacrificed everything that mattered for things that didn't. I'd enabled abuse. I'd abandoned my family. I'd destroyed my health. And I'd done it all while telling myself I was doing the right thing. That realization broke something in me. But it also freed me. Because once you stop lying to yourself, you can start living in truth.

LIVING WITHOUT DECEPTION

Living without deception is harder than living with it. Deception is comfortable. It protects you. It lets you avoid hard truths and difficult conversations. Deception lets you stay in situations that are destroying you because you can convince yourself they're not that bad. Deception lets you witness harm without doing anything because you can tell yourself it's not your responsibility. But living in truth—living without deception—requires constant vigilance. It requires being honest about your motivations. Why am I doing this? Is it because it's right, or because it's convenient? It requires being honest about your choices. Am I choosing this because it's good for me, or because I'm scared of the alternative? It requires being honest about your complicity. What am I enabling by my presence? What am I protecting by my silence? And it requires being honest about your failures. Where did I fall short? Who did I hurt? What do I need to make right? That's what living without deception looks like. And it's exhausting. But it's also freeing. Because when you're not carrying lies, you're lighter. When you're not protecting secrets, you're freer. When you're not hiding from truth, you're more at peace.

WORD IS BOND IN ACTION

So what does "Word is Bond: Built On No Deception" look like in practice? It means when I tell my daughter I'm going to show up, I show up. Not sometimes. Not when it's convenient. Every time. Because word is bond means keeping your commitments. Especially to the people who depend on you most. It means when young people ask me about my past, I tell them the truth. The whole truth. Not just the parts that make me look good. I tell them about the body I caught. The abuse I witnessed. The complicity I enabled. I tell them about the mistakes I made and the cost of those mistakes. Because word is bond means being honest even when honesty makes you look bad. It means when I talk about Puff, I tell the truth about both what I experienced and what I did. I don't just blame him for how he treated me. I take responsibility for staying. For enabling. For being complicit. I don't just talk about what he did wrong. I talk about what I did wrong. Because word is bond means taking full accountability for your choices. It means when I'm struggling, I say it. When I'm scared, I admit it. When I don't know something, I acknowledge it. Because word is bond means not pretending to be something you're not. It means when I make a mistake now, I own it immediately. I don't make excuses. I don't blame others. I don't minimize it. I say: "I was wrong. I'm sorry. Here's what I'm going to do differently." Because word is bond means taking responsibility instead of deflecting. It means when I teach young people, I don't just lecture them. I listen to them. I learn from them. I admit when they teach me something. Because word is bond means humility. Recognizing you don't have all the answers. It means when someone calls me out for something I did wrong, I don't get defensive. I listen. I reflect. And if they're right, I acknowledge it and change. Because word is bond means being willing to be wrong and grow from it. This is what living without deception looks like. And it's not easy. But it's right.

THE COST OF TRUTH

Living in truth cost me things. It cost me my relationship with Puff. Whatever was left of it. It cost me access to certain circles, certain opportunities. It cost me the approval of people who wanted me to stay silent. But you know what? I don't regret any of that. Because what I gained is worth more than what I lost. I gained my integrity. My self-respect. My peace. I gained honest relationships with my children. I gained purpose—knowing I'm using my story to help others. I gained freedom—from secrets, from lies, from complicity. And I gained something I never had before: the ability to look at myself in the mirror and respect the person looking back. That's priceless.

WHERE THINGS STAND NOW

As I write this, Puff is facing serious allegations and legal battles playing out publicly, and despite what many assume, I have never spoken to federal investigators, never been contacted by authorities, never taken the stand, and never testified for or against Sean Combs. What I did do was stop protecting silence. I chose to tell my truth publicly, in my own words, and only about what I personally witnessed and experienced. Not for revenge. Not to pile on. And not to celebrate anyone's downfall. I did it because accountability matters, and silence is how harm continues. Word is bond doesn't mean blind loyalty. It means standing on the side of truth, even when that truth is uncomfortable, even when it costs you, and even when it involves people you were once loyal to.

My son is still fighting his case in Africa. Thirteen years now. And we're still working on getting him home. That guilt hasn't gone away. The knowledge that I wasn't there for him when he needed me. That my choices contributed to his choices. But I'm showing up now in every way I can. Financially. Emotionally. Spiritually. I'm fighting for him. And when he comes home, I'll be there for him in ways I wasn't before. Because word is bond means showing up even when you've failed before.

My relationship with my older daughters is healing. Slowly. Painfully. But healing. They're seeing through my actions that I'm different now. That I prioritize them now. That I'm present now. We have hard conversations. About the past. About the pain. About what they needed and didn't get. And I listen. I acknowledge. I apologize. And I do better. Because word is bond means rebuilding trust through consistent action.

And Kennedi—my baby girl—is thriving. Eight months old now. Healthy. Happy. Beautiful. And I'm there for every moment. Every feeding. Every doctor's appointment. Every milestone. I'm being the father to her that I should've been to all my kids. And that doesn't erase what I missed with the others. But it shows them that I've changed. That I'm capable of being the father I should've been. Because word is bond means doing better, even if you can't undo the past.

My health is stable. PSA levels still low. Diabetes managed. Blood pressure under control. I go to every doctor's appointment. I take my medication. I exercise. I eat better. I manage my stress. Not perfectly. But consistently. Because word is bond means taking care of yourself so you can be there for others.

And my work—teaching young people, speaking about domestic violence, sharing my story—continues. Every week, I speak at schools, community centers, youth programs. Every week, young people reach out with questions, with struggles, with situations they're trying to navigate. Every week, I show up and tell the truth. Not because I'm a hero. Not because I've figured it all out. But because I have a story that can help others avoid the mistakes I made. And word is bond means using your experience to help others.

THE MESSAGE I WANT TO LEAVE

If you take nothing else from this book, take this: You don't have to repeat the cycles you were born into. I was born into poverty, violence, dysfunction. I saw my father abuse my mother. I saw the streets take everyone I looked up to. I learned that love looks like pain and loyalty looks like silence. And I repeated those patterns for fifty years. But I'm breaking them now. I'm showing my kids that men can be gentle. That fathers can be present. That strength includes vulnerability. I'm teaching young people that success doesn't mean proximity to power—it means building something real. I'm showing survivors of abuse that it's never too late to speak up. You can break the cycle. But it requires intention. Work. Honesty. It requires looking at the patterns you learned and deciding which ones to keep and which ones to reject.

You are not defined by your worst mistakes. I caught a body. I enabled abuse. I was complicit in harm. I abandoned my family. Those are facts. Parts of my story. Things I have to live with. But they're not all I am. I'm also someone who's trying to do better. Who's taking responsibility. Who's using my failures to help others. Your worst moment doesn't have to be your defining moment. You can grow. You can change. You can make amends. Not by hiding your mistakes. But by owning them and doing better.

Loyalty to the truth is more important than loyalty to people. I was loyal to Puff for twenty years. And that loyalty cost me everything. Because loyalty to the wrong person, loyalty that requires you to compromise yourself, loyalty that asks you to enable harm—that's not real loyalty. Real loyalty is being loyal to what's right. To the truth. To protecting the vulnerable. Even when it costs you. Even when people call you a traitor. Even when you lose everything. Because at the end of your life, you have to live with yourself. And you can't live with yourself if you betrayed your values to protect someone else.

Your word is everything. If you say you're going to do something, do it. If you make a promise, keep it. If you commit to change, follow through. Because trust is built through consistency. And once you lose people's trust, it's almost impossible to get it back. So guard your word. Protect your integrity. Build your life on truth. Because everything else—money, status, success—can be taken away. But your word, your integrity, your character—those are yours as long as you protect them.

It's never too late to tell the truth. I stayed silent for years. And that silence ate at me. But when I finally spoke up—when I finally told the truth about what I witnessed and what I did—I felt lighter. Not because everything was fixed. Not because I was forgiven. Not because the consequences went away. But because I was finally living in truth instead of deception. So if you're carrying secrets, if you're protecting people who hurt others, if you're living a lie—speak up. Tell the truth. Face the consequences. Do the right thing. It will cost you something. But staying silent will cost you more.

BUILT ON NO DECEPTION

This book is built on no deception. I didn't hide my failures. I didn't minimize my complicity. I didn't make myself the hero of a story where I was often the villain. I told the truth. About the streets. About violence. About Puff. About abuse. About my own failures. All of it. Not because I want sympathy. Not because I want to be forgiven. But because the only way to help others is to be honest about what you lived through. And that honesty—that commitment to living without deception—is what I'm building the rest of my life on. Every relationship. Every commitment. Every word I speak. Built on no deception.

That's what word is bond means to me now. Not just keeping your promises. But building your entire life on truth. Being honest about who you are, what you've done, where you've failed, and how you're trying to do better. Living in a way where your public self and your private self are aligned. Where you're not hiding anything. Where you're not pretending to be someone you're not. That's integrity. That's peace. That's freedom. And that's what I'm committed to for the rest of my life.

TO MY CHILDREN

To Roderick, my oldest: I'm sorry I wasn't there for you when you needed me most. I'm fighting for you now. And when you come home, I'll spend the rest of my life making it right. To my daughters—all five of you: I'm sorry I chose work over you. I'm sorry I was absent. I'm sorry I didn't give you the father you deserved. I can't change the past. But I'm showing up differently now. And I hope you can see that and, one day, forgive me. To Kennedi, my baby girl: You saved my life. You gave me a reason to live differently. To be better. To break the cycles I was trapped in. I promise you—word is bond—I will be the father you deserve. I will be present. I will protect you. I will teach you to live with integrity. And I will make sure the world you grow up in is better than the one I helped create.

TO THE YOUNG PEOPLE READING THIS

You don't have to make the mistakes I made. You don't have to learn everything the hard way. You can learn from my story. From my failures. From my pain. Choose different. Choose better. Choose truth. Don't chase proximity to power. Build your own power. Don't sacrifice your health for money. No amount of money is worth your life. Don't stay silent about abuse. Speak up. Intervene. Protect the vulnerable. Don't give loyalty to people who don't value you. Give loyalty to your values. Don't lie to yourself. Face the truth, even when it's uncomfortable. And build your life on truth. On integrity. On real relationships and real achievements. Build your life on no deception. Because that's the only foundation that lasts.

TO CASSIE AND ALL THE SURVIVORS

I'm sorry. I'm sorry I didn't do more. I'm sorry I stayed silent as long as I did. I'm sorry I protected my job over protecting you. I can't undo that. But I can make sure others don't make the same mistake. I'm speaking up now. I'm teaching men about accountability. I'm working with domestic violence organizations. I'm using my platform to make sure the next generation does better. It's not enough. But it's something. And I hope—I pray—that my willingness to finally tell the truth, to take responsibility, to use my story to help others, means something. Not for me. But for the people who come after us.

WORD IS BOND

This is my bond. My promise. My commitment. I will live the rest of my life in truth. I will speak up even when it costs me. I will take responsibility for my failures and use them to teach others. I will be present for my family. I will protect the vulnerable instead of the powerful. I will build everything I do on truth, not deception. Word is bond. Built on no deception. That's what my life is about now. Not success. Not money. Not status. But truth. Integrity. Making amends. Helping others. And I'm never going back to the man I was. Because that man was built on deception. Self-deception. Deception of others. Living a lie. But this man—the man I'm becoming—is built on truth. And even though truth is harder, even though it costs more, even though it's painful sometimes— It's worth it. Because this is the only way to actually live. Not just survive. Not just get by. Not just make it through. But actually live. With integrity. With peace. With purpose. That's what word is bond means. And that's what I'm committed to for the rest of my life. Built. On. No. Deception.

FINAL BOND CHECK

THE NEXT GENERATION

This is the last Bond Check. **The final lesson. The most important one.** And it's not about me. It's about you. More specifically, it's about what we're leaving behind. What we're teaching. What we're modeling. What we're passing down. Because whether we realize it or not, the next generation is watching. They're watching how we handle conflict. They're watching how we treat women. They're watching what we prioritize—money or family, status or integrity, power or truth. They're watching whether we speak up or stay silent. They're watching whether we take responsibility or make excuses. And they're learning.

WHAT THE NEXT GENERATION LEARNED FROM ME

For most of my life, I was teaching the next generation the wrong lessons. My son Roderick watched me catch a body. He watched me go to jail. He watched me come home and go back to the streets. And he learned: this is what men do. This is how you handle disrespect. This is what strength looks like. Now he's been locked up for thirteen years. Fighting a murder case. In Africa. Because he learned from me. My daughters watched me choose work over them. They watched me miss birthdays and graduations.

They watched me prioritize money over presence. And they learned: men aren't reliable. Fathers leave. Work is more important than family. That's what I taught them. Not with words. But with actions. Young men in my neighborhood watched me come home from jail respected. They watched me travel the world with Puff. They watched me have access to money and power. And they learned: proximity to power is success. The streets lead somewhere. Loyalty means silence. That's what I was teaching without even realizing it. Because the next generation doesn't just learn from what we say. They learn from what we do. How we live. The choices we make when no one's watching. And for fifty-six years, I was teaching all the wrong lessons.

WHAT I'M TEACHING NOW

But for the last two years—since cancer, since Kennedi, since I started speaking truth—I've been teaching different lessons. I'm teaching that real strength is vulnerability, not violence. That it's okay to cry. To admit when you're struggling. To ask for help. That being a man means taking responsibility, not avoiding it. I'm teaching that success is building your own, not working for someone else's. That proximity to power is a trap. That real power is ownership, equity, independence. That you can't sacrifice yourself for someone else's dream and call it success. I'm teaching that family is everything. That no amount of money is worth missing your kid's childhood. That being present is more important than being perfect. That your kids need your time more than your money. I'm teaching that silence is complicity. That if you see something wrong and don't speak up, you're part of the problem. That protecting the powerful over the vulnerable makes you complicit in their harm. That speaking up will cost you something, but staying silent will cost you more. I'm teaching that redemption is possible. That you can mess up and still make things right. That it's never too late to change, to tell the truth, to do better. That your worst moment doesn't have to define you if you do the work to grow. These are the lessons I'm teaching now. Not perfectly. But consistently. Not through words alone. But through action. Because the next generation is still watching.

WHAT THE NEXT GENERATION NEEDS FROM US

The next generation doesn't need us to be perfect. They need us to be honest. They don't need us to have all the answers. They need us to be willing to admit when we don't. They don't need us to be heroes. They need us to be human. They need us to: Tell the truth about our failures. Not hide them. Not minimize them. But own them. Tell them what we did wrong. What it cost. What we wish we'd done differently. Because they can learn from our mistakes. But only if we're honest about them. Model accountability. When we mess up—and we will—own it. Apologize. Make it right. Don't make excuses. Don't blame others. Don't deflect. Because they're learning how to handle their own mistakes by watching how we handle ours. Show them healthy masculinity. Show them that men can be gentle and strong. That men can cry and still be respected. That men can ask for help and still be leaders. That men can be emotionally available without being weak. Because toxic masculinity is killing our sons. And we're the ones who can change that. Teach them about consent and respect. Teach them that no means no. That silence isn't consent. That power dynamics matter. Teach them that women aren't objects or conquests. Teach them that real men protect women, they don't abuse them. Because the next generation of men needs to do better than we did. Show them what healthy relationships look like. Not perfect relationships. But honest ones. Relationships with boundaries. With communication. With mutual respect. Relationships where both people feel safe, valued, heard. Because many of us didn't see healthy relationships growing up. So we have to model them now. Teach them financial literacy. Teach them the difference between making money and building wealth. Teach them about ownership, equity, investments. Teach them not to work for someone else's dream their whole life. Because we want them to build something real. Not just survive. Teach them to speak up. Teach them that silence in the face of injustice is complicity. That loyalty to people is less important than loyalty to what's right. That speaking up will cost them something, but it's worth it. Because the world needs more people who speak up, not more people who stay silent to protect themselves. Teach them to break cycles. Teach them that just because something happened to us doesn't mean it has to happen to them. That they can choose different. Be different. Do different. That cycles can be broken, but it takes intention and work. Because we don't want them to repeat our mistakes. We want them to learn from them and do better.

THE RESPONSIBILITY WE CARRY

Every adult carries a responsibility to the next generation. Whether you have kids or not. Whether you work with young people or not. We all have a responsibility. Because young people are watching all of us. They're watching how we treat service workers. They're watching how we talk about women. They're watching how we handle conflict. They're watching what we prioritize. They're watching whether our words match our actions. And they're learning. So we have to ask ourselves: What am I teaching through how I live? Am I teaching that money is more important than integrity? Am I teaching that power is more important than compassion? Am I teaching that winning is more important than doing what's right? Or am I teaching that integrity matters more than success?

That compassion matters more than status? That doing what's right matters more than winning? Because our actions teach whether we intend them to or not.

THE STAKES

The stakes couldn't be higher. We're seeing the consequences of what my generation taught—or failed to teach—the generation after us. We're seeing young men who think violence is the only answer to disrespect. We're seeing young women who normalize abuse because they've never seen healthy relationships. We're seeing kids chasing proximity to power instead of building their own. We're seeing people prioritize money over everything else and wondering why they're empty. We're seeing silence in the face of injustice because people are scared to speak up. That's what happens when we fail to teach the right lessons. But we can change that. Not for our generation—we made our choices. But for the next one. We can teach them different. Show them different. Model different. We can break the cycles we were trapped in. We can correct the lessons we learned wrong. We can do better than the generation before us did. But only if we commit to it.

FOR THE PARENTS READING THIS

If you're a parent, you have the most direct impact. Your kids are watching you every day. They're watching how you treat your partner. They're watching how you handle stress. They're watching what you prioritize when you're tired or overwhelmed. They're watching whether you keep your promises. They're watching how you talk about other people. And they're learning what's normal. What's acceptable. What's expected. So ask yourself: What am I modeling for my kids? Are you showing them that work is more important than them? Are you showing them that men don't show emotions? Are you showing them that conflict gets resolved through violence or through communication? Are you showing them that women should be controlled or respected? Are you showing them that mistakes should be hidden or owned? Your kids are going to become who you are, not who you tell them to be. So if you want them to do better than you did, you have to do better yourself. You have to be present. Be honest. Be accountable. You have to show them what healthy looks like. You have to apologize when you mess up. You have to prioritize them over work, money, status. Because they're watching. And they're learning. And the lessons you teach them now will shape the rest of their lives.

FOR THE YOUNG PEOPLE READING THIS

If you're part of the next generation, this is for you: You don't have to repeat the mistakes of the generation before you. You can look at what we did wrong and choose different. You can look at the pain we caused and decide not to cause that pain. You can look at the cycles we perpetuated and decide to break them. You have a choice. You can choose to: Resolve conflict through communication, not violence. Build your own empire instead of working for someone else's. Speak up when you see something wrong. Be present for your family. Show vulnerability instead of pretending to be tough. Take responsibility instead of making excuses. Protect the vulnerable instead of the powerful. Live with integrity instead of chasing status. These choices won't always be easy. They'll cost you something. But they're worth it. Because the life you build with these choices will be real. Not perfect. But real. Not easy. But meaningful. Not glamorous. But sustainable. And that's what you deserve. Not a life that looks good from the outside but destroys you from the inside. But a life that you can actually be proud of.

FOR KENNEDI

My baby girl. You're eight months old as I write this. You can't read this yet. But one day you will. And when you do, I want you to know: You saved my life. Not metaphorically. Literally. You gave me a reason to change when I didn't think I could. You gave me a reason to speak truth when it was easier to stay silent. You gave me a reason to prioritize what actually matters. Before you, I was dying. Not just physically, but spiritually. I was carrying secrets that were eating me alive. I was living a lie and calling it success. I was repeating cycles I should've broken. But when you were born, everything changed. Because I looked at you and thought: In eighteen years, she's going to be the age Cassie was when she met Puff. And I need to make sure the world she grows up in is different. I need to make sure men like me speak up instead of staying silent. I need to make sure the next generation learns different lessons than I learned. So I chose truth. Even when it cost me. I chose speaking up. Even when people called me a snitch. I chose integrity. Even when it meant losing everything else. Because you deserve a father who lives with integrity. You deserve a world where powerful men are held accountable. You deserve to grow up learning healthy lessons, not toxic ones. And I'm going to spend the rest of my life making sure you have that. Word is bond, baby girl. I'm going to be present. I'm going to be honest. I'm going to be the father you deserve. I'm going to teach you that your worth isn't based on what men think of you. I'm going to teach you to speak up, to set boundaries, to walk away from anything that doesn't serve you. I'm going to teach you that real love never hurts. That respect is non-negotiable. That you deserve to be treated well. And I'm going to model that by how I live. By how I treat your mother. By how I treat women. By how I handle conflict. By being accountable. By being vulnerable. By being present.

Because you're watching. And you're learning. And I'm never going back to being the man I was.

THE COMMITMENT WE MUST MAKE

This is the commitment I'm making to the next generation: I will tell the truth about my failures so you can learn from them. I will take responsibility for my complicity so you understand accountability. I will speak up about injustice so you know silence isn't an option. I will be present for my family so you see what that looks like. I will show vulnerability so you know strength includes admitting weakness. I will live with integrity so you see it's possible even after failure. That's my commitment. And I'm asking you—everyone reading this—to make the same commitment. Commit to teaching the next generation better lessons than we learned. Commit to modeling healthy behavior even when it's hard. Commit to breaking cycles even when no one else in your family has. Commit to speaking up even when it costs you. Commit to being present even when you're tired. Commit to being honest even when lies are easier. Because the next generation deserves better than what we got. They deserve fathers who are present. They deserve to see healthy relationships. They deserve to learn that success means integrity, not just money. They deserve to know that speaking up is strength, not weakness. They deserve to be taught that they can break cycles, not just repeat them. And we're the ones who have to teach them. Not perfectly. We're going to mess up. We're going to fall short sometimes. But consistently. Honestly. With intention. That's all we can do. Show up. Tell the truth. Model integrity. Teach better lessons. And trust that even though we can't control outcomes, we can influence them.

THE HOPE I HOLD

I have hope for the next generation. Not because they're perfect. But because they have access to information we didn't. They're asking questions we were too scared to ask. They're challenging norms we accepted without thinking. They're demanding accountability we never demanded. And they're watching us. Watching to see if we're willing to tell the truth. Watching to see if we're willing to take responsibility. Watching to see if we're willing to change. And when they see us do that—when they see us be honest about our failures, take accountability, do better—it gives them permission to do the same. That's how cycles break. Not by pretending the previous generation was perfect. But by acknowledging where they failed and choosing to do different. So I have hope. Hope that my son will come home and be better than I was. Hope that my daughters will choose partners who treat them better than I treated people. Hope that Kennedi will grow up in a world where men speak up instead of staying silent. Hope that the young people I teach will make better choices than I made. That hope is what keeps me going.

THE FINAL LESSON

Here's the final lesson. The most important one. The next generation will inherit whatever we leave behind. If we leave behind silence, they'll inherit more abuse. If we leave behind toxic masculinity, they'll inherit more violence. If we leave behind complicity, they'll inherit more injustice. If we leave behind broken families, they'll inherit more dysfunction. But if we leave behind truth, they'll inherit accountability. If we leave behind healthy models of masculinity, they'll inherit peace. If we leave behind courage to speak up, they'll inherit justice. If we leave behind present fathers, they'll inherit healed families. What we do now determines what they inherit. So we have a choice. We can protect our comfort, our secrets, our complicity. We can stay silent to protect ourselves. We can keep repeating the same cycles. Or we can do the hard work of change. We can speak truth even when it costs us. We can break the cycles we were born into. That's the choice. And I'm choosing the second path. Not because I'm better than anyone. Not because I've figured it all out. But because I have a baby girl who's watching. And I have young people who need to hear that change is possible. And I have a generation behind me that deserves better than what I gave them for fifty-six years. So I'm doing the work. Telling the truth. Taking responsibility. Being present. Teaching better lessons. And I'm inviting you to do the same. For the next generation. For your kids. Your nieces and nephews. The young people in your community. For Kennedi and every other child who deserves to grow up in a world that's better than the one we created. Let's break the cycles. Let's teach better lessons. Let's leave behind truth instead of deception. Because the next generation is watching. And they deserve better. Word is bond. Built on no deception. For the next generation.

EPILOGUE

A LETTER TO MY YOUNGER SELF

Dear Bonds,

I'm writing to you from forty-four years in the future.
I'm fifty-eight now. You're fourteen, standing on the corner of 155th Street in Polo Grounds, trying to decide who you're going to be.

I know what you're thinking.

You're watching the guy who just pulled up in the BMW, Gucci outfit, rope chain shining. Everybody respects him. Girls love him. He looks like he made it. You want that. You want to matter.

I get it.

Mom and Pops are fighting again. You heard him hit her. You heard her cry. You feel powerless. Invisible. Angry. You want respect, control, a way out. And that guy in the BMW looks like proof that the streets work.

So you're thinking about asking him to put you on.

I'm writing to tell you: you're wrong.

But I know you won't listen. I didn't. Not when Mom begged me to stay in school. Not when teachers told me I had potential. Not when older heads warned me we were all going nowhere. I thought I knew better. I was hurt, angry, and desperate to be somebody.

So I'll say it anyway. In case some part of you hears it later.

Here's the truth.

That guy in the BMW will be dead before you're twenty-five. Shot over a deal gone wrong. The man you're about to work for will do twenty-five years in federal prison. His kids will grow up without him. His girl will leave. He'll come home old, broke, and forgotten.

That's where this path goes.
Not success. Not respect.
Death or prison.

You'll tell yourself you'll be different. Smarter. In and out.

I told myself that too.

At first, it works. You get money. People respect you. Girls want you. You finally feel seen. But then you start seeing things you can't unsee. Doing things you can't undo.

At nineteen, you'll take a life. You'll carry that weight forever. You'll dream about his face. You'll wonder about his family. And no amount of money will make that go away.

You'll go to jail. More than once. You'll miss years. Miss your kids growing up. Miss moments you can never get back.

And when you think you're done with the streets, you'll fall into a different trap.

You'll work for a powerful man. Famous. Rich. And you'll think being close to his power makes you powerful. You'll give him twenty years of your life.

He'll take your health. Your marriage. Your relationship with your kids. Your peace. Your integrity. And when you're no longer useful, he'll discard you without a second thought.

At fifty-eight, you'll have diabetes, high blood pressure, cancer. Six kids who barely know you. Regrets that don't let you sleep.

That's where this path ends.

I know you won't listen. Pain and anger are louder than warnings. So if you're going to walk this road anyway, hear this:

Don't lose yourself completely.

When that voice inside tells you something isn't right, listen. That's your conscience. Don't kill it.

When you catch that body, turn yourself in. Running will eat you alive. Taking responsibility is the first step toward becoming a man.

Don't stay loyal to the wrong people. Most will use you and disappear. Pay attention to who shows up when things fall apart. Those are your real ones.

When you have kids, be there. Money isn't enough. Presence matters. Your absence will echo in their lives. One of your sons will follow your footsteps because you weren't there to show him another way. That guilt will never leave you.

When you see abuse, speak up. Silence costs more than you think. I stayed silent. I live with that.

Take care of your health. Stress, no sleep, trauma will catch up to you. I almost died waiting too long.

The streets don't love you back. They'll take everything and keep moving. Have an exit plan. Build something else. Learn something else.

You are not your environment. Polo Grounds isn't your destiny. You're smart. Capable. You could build something real if you believed you were allowed to.

It's never too late to change. You can make terrible mistakes and still become a good man. But change takes humility, honesty, and work. Harder work than the streets.

Real success isn't money or status. It's peace. Integrity. Your kids being proud of you. Being able to look in the mirror and respect what you see.

What I know now is simple: the things I chased didn't matter. The things I ignored did.

At fifty-eight, I'm choosing differently. I'm present for Kennedi. I'm telling the truth. I'm teaching others. I'm rebuilding what I broke. I'm living with integrity.

I have more peace now than I ever did with money and status. Because peace comes from who you are, not what you have.

If I could stand next to you on that corner, I'd tell you this:

You're enough. You don't need chains or a BMW to be worthy. Your anger makes sense, but hurting others won't heal you. Ask for help. Process your pain. Choose the harder path. It leads somewhere real.

And I'd tell you I love you.

I forgive you for everything you're going to do wrong. You were just a hurt kid trying to survive.

This letter isn't really for you. I can't go back.

It's for every kid standing on a corner right now thinking the streets are the only option.

They're not.

You always have a choice. Even when it doesn't feel like one.

Choose integrity over money. Presence over absence. Truth over deception. Health over hustling. Building over destroying.

The path I chose cost me everything that mattered.

I don't want you to pay the same price.

Forty-four years later, all I can do is move forward and tell the truth.

And maybe that fourteen-year-old kid would be proud of the man I'm becoming—not because I'm successful, but because I'm finally living with integrity.

Word is bond. Built on no deception.

That's my promise.
 And I'm keeping it.

— Bonds

FRAMEWORK FOR CHANGE

A PRACTICAL GUIDE TO BREAKING CYCLES AND BUILDING INTEGRITY

This isn't just my story. It's a mirror. And if you're reading this, you probably saw something in my story that looks familiar.

Maybe you saw yourself in the streets, making choices you know will cost you later. Maybe you saw yourself in a toxic job, sacrificing everything for someone who doesn't value you. Maybe you saw yourself staying silent when you should speak up. Maybe you saw yourself repeating cycles you promised you'd break.

This framework is for you.

It's not going to fix everything overnight. Change doesn't work like that. But it will give you a map. A starting point. A way forward.

Because I know what it's like to want to change but not know how. To feel stuck. To feel trapped. To feel like there's no way out.

But there is.

And this framework—**Word Is Bond: Built On No Deception**—is how you start.

THE B.O.N.D. FRAMEWORK

B - Be Honest (Assessment)
O - Own Your Part (Accountability)
N - Name What Needs to Change (Action Plan)
D - Do the Work (Implementation)

Let me walk you through each step.

STEP ONE: BE HONEST (ASSESSMENT)

The first step is the hardest: being brutally honest with yourself.

Not the story you tell other people. Not the version that makes you look good.

The truth.

THE TRUTH ABOUT YOUR SITUATION

Grab a piece of paper. Or open a note on your phone. Whatever works.

Answer these questions honestly. Nobody's going to see this but you.

CURRENT STATE ASSESSMENT

1. **What am I doing that I know is wrong?**
   - Not "kind of wrong" or "depends how you look at it"
   - What am I doing that I KNOW is wrong?
   - Write it down. All of it.
2. **Who am I hurting?**
   - Myself?
   - My family?
   - My partner?
   - My kids?
   - Others?
   - Be specific.
3. **What lies am I telling myself?**
   - "I don't have a choice"
   - "It's not that bad"
   - "I'll change later"
   - "They deserve it"
   - "This is just temporary"
   - What lies are you using to justify your choices?
4. **What am I sacrificing?**
   - Health?
   - Relationships?
   - Integrity?

□ Peace?

□ Time?

□ What's this costing you that you're pretending it's not?

5. **If I keep going this way, where will I be in 5 years? 10 years?**

□ Not where you hope to be

□ Where you'll actually be if nothing changes

□ Be realistic

6. **What would I tell my child if they were in my situation?**

□ If your son or daughter was doing exactly what you're doing, what would you tell them?

□ Now ask yourself: Why am I not taking that advice?

THE TRUTH ABOUT YOUR PATTERNS

Now look at your answers and identify patterns.

PATTERN RECOGNITION

1. **Is this the first time I've been in a situation like this?**

□ Or is this a pattern?

□ Different people, different places, but same dynamic?

2. **What cycle am I repeating?**

□ From my childhood?

□ From my family?

□ From my past?

□ What am I doing that was done to me or that I saw growing up?

3. **What am I avoiding by staying in this situation?**

□ Change?

- ☐ Uncertainty?
- ☐ Responsibility?
- ☐ Loneliness?
- ☐ Starting over?
- ☐ What's the fear underneath the choice to stay?

4. **What story am I telling myself about why I can't change?**
   - ☐ "I'm too old"
   - ☐ "I don't have options"
   - ☐ "Nobody will hire me"
   - ☐ "I need the money"
   - ☐ "They need me"
   - ☐ What's your story? And is it true or is it an excuse?

THE TRUTH TEST

For each answer you wrote, ask yourself:

"If my child came to me with this exact situation, would I tell them to stay or leave?"

If the answer is leave, then you already know what you need to do.

The question isn't whether you should leave. It's what's stopping you.

And that's what we address in the next steps.

STEP TWO: OWN YOUR PART (ACCOUNTABILITY)

This is where most people get stuck.

Because it's easier to blame other people than to look at yourself.

But you can't change what you don't own.

TAKE FULL RESPONSIBILITY

Answer these questions:

ACCOUNTABILITY ASSESSMENT

1. **What role did I play in getting here?**
   - ☐ Not what others did to you
   - ☐ What choices did YOU make that led here?
   - ☐ Even if you were young. Even if you didn't know better. Even if others influenced you.
   - ☐ What part did you play?
2. **What warning signs did I ignore?**
   - ☐ What did I see early on that I dismissed?
   - ☐ What red flags did I rationalize?
   - ☐ When did I know something was wrong but stayed anyway?
3. **Who did I hurt by my choices?**
   - ☐ Be specific

      ☐ Include yourself on this list

4. What did I know was wrong but did anyway?

      ☐ What did your conscience tell you not to do?

      ☐ What did you do despite knowing better?

5. What am I still making excuses for?

      ☐ Where am I still minimizing?

      ☐ Where am I still blaming others?

      ☐ Where am I still not taking full responsibility?

6. If someone did to my child what I did to others, how would I feel?

      ☐ If someone treated your kid the way you treated people, what would you want for them?

      ☐ Justice? Accountability? Change?

      ☐ Why aren't you holding yourself to that standard?

WRITE YOUR ACCOUNTABILITY STATEMENT

Now write out, in your own words:

"I take full responsibility for:

      ☐ [List what you're accountable for]

I acknowledge that:

      ☐ [What you now understand about the impact of your choices]

I can't change what I did, but I can:

☐   [What you're going to do differently going forward]"

This isn't for anyone else. This is for you.

To see it written out. To own it. To stop running from it.

WHO DESERVES ACKNOWLEDGMENT?

Make a list of people you've hurt or failed.

You don't have to reach out to them yet (we'll get to that).

But write down:

AMENDS LIST

1. **Name:**
2. **What I did or didn't do:**
3. **How it affected them:**
4. **What making amends looks like (if possible):**

Some people you can't make amends to. They've passed. They've moved on. They don't want contact.

That's okay. You can still acknowledge what you did and commit to doing better.

STEP THREE: NAME WHAT NEEDS TO CHANGE (ACTION PLAN)

Now that you've been honest and taken accountability, it's time to get specific about what needs to change.

IDENTIFY YOUR NON-NEGOTIABLES

These are the things that MUST change. Not "should" change. Not "it would be nice if" they changed.

MUST change.

NON-NEGOTIABLE CHANGES

Write down:

1. **What must I stop doing immediately?**
   - ☐ What behavior is actively harming you or others?
   - ☐ What can't continue even one more day?
2. **What must I start doing immediately?**
   - ☐ What do you need to start right now?
   - ☐ What can't wait?
3. **Who must I distance myself from?**
   - ☐ Who is toxic to your growth?
   - ☐ Who enables your worst behaviors?

☐ Who will pull you back if you try to change?

4. **What environment must I leave?**

☐ What physical space is keeping you stuck?

☐ Where do you need to remove yourself from?

5. **What help do I need that I've been refusing?**

☐ Therapy?

☐ Rehab?

☐ Financial counseling?

☐ Medical attention?

☐ What professional help have you been avoiding?

CREATE YOUR EXIT STRATEGY

If you're in a toxic situation—job, relationship, lifestyle—you need an exit strategy.

EXIT PLANNING WORKSHEET

1. **What am I exiting from?**

☐ Be specific

2. **What's keeping me here?**

☐ Money?

☐ Fear?

☐ Loyalty?

☐ Identity?

☐ Lack of options?

☐ Be honest about the real reasons

3. **What do I need in place before I can leave?**

☐ Savings?

☐ Another job?

- ☐ Housing?
- ☐ Support system?
- ☐ Be realistic but don't let "perfect conditions" become an excuse to never leave

4. **What's my timeline?**
   - ☐ Not "someday"
   - ☐ Actual dates
   - ☐ What happens this week? This month? In 3 months? In 6 months?

5. **What's my backup plan if things go wrong?**
   - ☐ Where can I stay if I need to leave suddenly?
   - ☐ Who can I call?
   - ☐ What resources are available?

6. **What's my "I'm leaving" line?**
   - ☐ What condition, if it happens, means you leave immediately?
   - ☐ No more second chances. No more "one more time."
   - ☐ What's your hard line?

Example:

- ☐ "If he puts his hands on me again, I'm leaving that day"
- ☐ "If my health gets worse, I'm quitting that week"
- ☐ "If I'm asked to do something illegal, I'm walking out immediately"

Write yours down. And stick to it.

BUILD YOUR SUPPORT SYSTEM

You can't do this alone.

SUPPORT SYSTEM MAPPING

Identify:

1. **Who can I talk to honestly?**
   - ☐ Who won't judge but will hold you accountable?
   - ☐ Who will support your change?
2. **What professional help do I need?**
   - ☐ Therapist?
   - ☐ Counselor?
   - ☐ Sponsor?
   - ☐ Coach?
   - ☐ Financial advisor?
   - ☐ Doctor?
3. **What resources are available to me?**
   - ☐ Community programs?
   - ☐ Support groups?
   - ☐ Hotlines?
   - ☐ Organizations?
   - ☐ Do the research. Write down actual names, numbers, addresses.
4. **Who do I need to tell about my plan?**
   - ☐ Who needs to know you're making changes?
   - ☐ Who will help keep you accountable?

SET CLEAR BOUNDARIES

Part of change is setting boundaries you've never set before.

BOUNDARY SETTING

For each relationship or situation, identify:

1. **What I will no longer accept:**
   - ☐ Be specific
   - ☐ "Disrespect" is vague. "Being yelled at" is specific.
2. **What I will do if that boundary is crossed:**
   - ☐ Not threats. Consequences.
   - ☐ What will you actually do?
   - ☐ "I will leave the room"
   - ☐ "I will end the conversation"
   - ☐ "I will file a report"
   - ☐ "I will leave the relationship"
3. **What I need to communicate clearly:**
   - ☐ People aren't mind readers
   - ☐ What do you need to tell people about your boundaries?

STEP FOUR: DO THE WORK (IMPLEMENTATION)

This is where theory becomes action.

Where plans become life changes.

This is the hardest part. Because it requires sustained effort. Daily choices. Consistent action.

DAILY PRACTICES

Change happens through daily discipline, not one-time decisions.

THE DAILY INTEGRITY CHECK

Every night before bed, ask yourself:

1. **Did I live with integrity today?**
   - ☐ Not perfection. Integrity.
   - ☐ Did my actions match my values?
2. **Where did I compromise myself today?**
   - ☐ Where did I do something I knew was wrong?
   - ☐ Where did I stay silent when I should've spoken?
   - ☐ Where did I prioritize comfort over what's right?
3. **What will I do differently tomorrow?**
   - ☐ Specific. Actionable.
   - ☐ Not "be better." But "speak up in that meeting" or "set that boundary with my partner."

THE MORNING COMMITMENT

Every morning, before you start your day:

1. **What are my non-negotiables today?**
   - ☐ What boundaries am I protecting?

- ☐ What am I not compromising on?

2. **What's one thing I can do today that moves me toward change?**
    - ☐ Make one phone call?
    - ☐ Have one conversation?
    - ☐ Apply to one job?
    - ☐ One thing. Every day.

3. **Who do I need to be today to become who I want to be?**
    - ☐ Not who you've been. Who you're becoming.
    - ☐ What does that person do? Be that today.

WEEKLY CHECK-INS

Every week, assess your progress.

WEEKLY PROGRESS ASSESSMENT

1. **What did I do this week that I'm proud of?**
    - ☐ Acknowledge progress, even small progress
2. **Where did I fall short?**
    - ☐ No judgment. Just observation.
    - ☐ What happened? Why?
3. **What pattern am I noticing?**
    - ☐ What keeps tripping me up?
    - ☐ What's the common thread in my struggles?
4. **What do I need to adjust?**
    - ☐ What's not working?
    - ☐ What needs to change about my approach?
5. **What support do I need that I'm not getting?**

☐   Do I need to reach out to someone?

☐   Do I need to find a resource I don't have yet?

MONTHLY MILESTONE REVIEWS

Once a month, do a deeper assessment.

MONTHLY MILESTONE CHECK

1. **What's changed in the last 30 days?**
   ☐   In your situation?
   ☐   In your mindset?
   ☐   In your actions?

2. **What's still the same that needs to change?**
   ☐   What are you still tolerating that you said you wouldn't?
   ☐   What adjustments need to be made?

3. **Am I on track with my exit strategy/change plan?**
   ☐   If not, why not?
   ☐   What needs to be adjusted?

4. **What new insights do I have?**
   ☐   What have I learned about myself?
   ☐   What have I learned about change?

5. **What's my focus for the next 30 days?**
   ☐   What's the one thing that will make the biggest difference?

WHEN YOU FALL SHORT (BECAUSE YOU WILL)

Change isn't linear. You're going to mess up. You're going to fall back into old patterns sometimes.

That doesn't mean you've failed. It means you're human.

THE FALLING SHORT PROTOCOL

When you mess up:

1. **Acknowledge it immediately**
   - ☐ Don't minimize it
   - ☐ Don't make excuses
   - ☐ Just acknowledge: "I messed up."
2. **Identify what happened**
   - ☐ What triggered it?
   - ☐ What was the situation?
   - ☐ What choice did you make?
3. **Take responsibility**
   - ☐ If you hurt someone, make it right
   - ☐ If you broke a commitment, acknowledge it
   - ☐ No excuses. Just accountability.
4. **Learn from it**
   - ☐ What do you need to do differently next time?
   - ☐ What boundary do you need to set?
   - ☐ What support do you need?
5. **Recommit**
   - ☐ Falling doesn't mean quitting

- ☐ Get back up
- ☐ Recommit to the change you're making

Remember: Setbacks are part of the process. What matters is what you do after.

THE WORD IS BOND CONTRACT

This is your commitment to yourself.

Fill this out. Sign it. Date it. Keep it somewhere you'll see it.

MY WORD IS BOND CONTRACT

I, _____, **commit to living Built On No Deception.**

I acknowledge that:

- ☐ I have made choices that hurt myself and others
- ☐ I cannot change the past, but I can change my future
- ☐ Change will require daily work and sustained effort
- ☐ I will fall short sometimes, but I will not quit
- ☐ I am responsible for the life I build from here forward

I commit to:

1. Being honest with myself about:

_____

2. **Taking accountability for:**

_____

3. **Leaving/changing:** _____

4. **Building:** _____

5. **Protecting these non-negotiables:**

_____

I will measure my progress by:

- ☐ _____ (specific, measurable goal)
- ☐ _____ (specific, measurable goal)
- ☐ _____ (specific, measurable goal)

My timeline:

- ☐ **In 30 days, I will:** _____
- ☐ **In 90 days, I will:** _____
- ☐ **In 6 months, I will:** _____
- ☐ **In 1 year, I will:** _____

My accountability partners are:

1.

When I want to quit, I will remember:

Signed: _____

Date: _____

Witnessed by (optional): _____

RESOURCES FOR CHANGE

You're not alone. There are people and organizations who can help.

FOR DOMESTIC VIOLENCE

National Domestic Violence Hotline

- ☐ 1-800-799-7233
- ☐ Text START to 88788
- ☐ Available 24/7
- ☐ www.thehotline.org

FOR MENTAL HEALTH

National Suicide Prevention Lifeline

- ☐ 988 (call or text)
- ☐ Available 24/7

SAMHSA National Helpline (Substance Abuse and Mental Health)

- □ 1-800-662-4357
- □ Available 24/7
- □ Treatment referral and information service

Psychology Today Therapist Finder

- □ www.psychologytoday.com/us/therapists
- □ Find therapists by location, insurance, specialty

FOR FORMERLY INCARCERATED INDIVIDUALS

National Reentry Resource Center

- □ www.nationalreentryresourcecenter.org
- □ Employment, housing, and support resources

Prison Fellowship

- □ 1-800-206-9764
- □ Reentry support and mentoring

FOR ADDICTION

Alcoholics Anonymous

- □ www.aa.org
- □ Find local meetings

Narcotics Anonymous

- ☐ www.na.org
- ☐ Find local meetings

SMART Recovery

- ☐ www.smartrecovery.org
- ☐ Science-based addiction recovery support

FOR EMPLOYMENT

American Job Centers

- ☐ www.careeronestop.org
- ☐ Free job training and placement services

Goodwill Career Services

- ☐ www.goodwill.org
- ☐ Job training, especially for those with barriers to employment

FOR FINANCIAL HELP

National Foundation for Credit Counseling

- ☐ 1-800-388-2227
- ☐ www.nfcc.org
- ☐ Free or low-cost financial counseling

FOR YOUTH

Boys & Girls Clubs of America

- ☐ www.bgca.org
- ☐ Mentoring and youth development programs

National Runaway Safeline

- ☐ 1-800-786-2929
- ☐ Available 24/7

FINAL WORDS

This framework works. But only if you work it. It's not magic. It's not easy. It's not overnight. It's daily choices, sustained effort, consistent action. It's falling down and getting back up. It's being honest even when it hurts. It's taking responsibility even when it's hard. It's doing the right thing even when it costs you. That's how change happens.

I know because I've lived it. At fifty-eight, I'm finally living with integrity. I'm finally speaking truth. I'm finally being the man I should've been all along. And if I can do it after fifty-six years of doing it wrong, you can too. No matter where you are. No matter what you've done. No matter how stuck you feel. Change is possible.

But you have to choose it. And you have to work for it. And you have to commit to it even when it's hard. Word is bond. Built on no deception.

That's the path forward. And I'll be walking it with you. Not ahead of you. Not behind you. But beside you.

Because we're all works in progress. We're all trying to do better than we did yesterday. We're all trying to break cycles and build something real. So let's do it together. One day at a time. One choice at a time. One step at a time. Built on no deception.

Let's go.

— **Bonds**

ACKNOWLEDGMENTS

First and foremost, I **thank God** for keeping me alive long enough to tell this story. There were countless moments when I shouldn't have made it. Bullets that missed. Decisions that could have buried me. A lifestyle that was slowly killing me. But I'm still here. And I know that's not by accident.

To my mother: I'm sorry for everything I put you through. You didn't deserve to watch your son choose the streets or spend nights wondering if I'd make it home. Thank you for never giving up on me, even when I had given up on myself. I love you more than I've ever been able to put into words.

To my children, all six of you: you are my greatest accomplishment. Kevan, Cydney, T'Nyah, Paige, Keke, and Kennedi.
To my oldest, who's been fighting his own battles, I see you. I'm proud of you.
To my daughters, you taught me more about being a man than the streets ever could.
And to my baby girl, Kennedi: Daddy is committed to making sure the world you grow up in is better than the one I came from.

To my ex-wife: twenty-five years is a long time to stand beside someone who wasn't always standing right. You held it down when I was locked up, when I was chasing someone else's dream, and through everything in between. I'm sorry for the pain I caused. Thank you for the years you gave me, and for never turning my kids against me.

To the Ciroc Boyz South—my brothers who helped me move cases, stay busy, and stay booked from Atlanta all the way to Dubai—your work, loyalty, and hustle will never be forgotten. What we built together was real, and I'll always respect the role you played in that chapter of my life.

To my OGs who kept me from self-destructing: you saw something in me I couldn't see in myself. Every time you checked me, redirected me, or stopped me from doing something stupid, you saved my life. This book exists because you cared enough to intervene.

To Stan: since we were fourteen years old in the Polo Grounds, you've been my brother. You gave me the name "Bonds," and you understood me when nobody else did. Even when life took us in different directions, that bond never broke.

To Big Dave, Tito Johnson, and all the real ones who showed me there was a code to this: you taught me that respect isn't just about fear. It's about character. About how you carry yourself and who you stand up for when it matters.

To the young brothers I mentor: you teach me every time we talk. You remind me why this book matters. Your struggles are real. Your pain is valid. And your future is not determined by your past. Keep fighting.

To everyone who survived the life I'm writing about—whether you were in the streets with me, in the industry with me, or caught in the chaos I sometimes caused—I see you. Your story matters too. I hope mine helps you tell yours.

To Ash Cash: you didn't just help me write this book, you helped me find my voice. You took hours of conversations, decades of memories, and a lifetime of lessons and helped me shape them into something that can actually help people. You never tried to make me sound like anyone but myself. Thank you for your patience, your skill, and your commitment to getting this right.

To Cassie, and to all the women who suffered in silence: I'm sorry I didn't do more. I'm sorry I normalized what should have never been normal. Speaking up now doesn't erase my silence then, but I hope it helps prevent the next young woman from believing she has to endure abuse to achieve her dreams.

To my doctors: thank you for catching my cancer early and for telling me the truth about how I was living. Diabetes, cancer, and everything my body went through were warnings. I'm finally listening.

To everyone trapped in toxic situations because you think you have no options: you do. This book is proof that it's never too late to choose yourself, to tell the truth, and to start building something real.

This book is dedicated to everyone dealing with domestic violence who feels like they have nowhere to go and no one to turn to. You are not alone.

And finally, to anyone who's ever felt like they had to compromise who they are just to make it:
Word is bond—built on no deception.
That's not just a saying. That's how I'm choosing to live now. The shortcut always costs more than you think. Do it the right way, even when it's harder. Your integrity is everything.

This book is my truth. It's not pretty. It's not perfect. And it doesn't make me a hero. But it's real. And if it helps even one person avoid my mistakes, leave a situation that's killing them, or believe their past doesn't have to define their future—then every hard conversation and painful memory was worth it.

Word is bond.

— **Roger "Bonds" Rowan**

ABOUT THE AUTHOR

Roger "Bonds" Rowan is a survivor, storyteller, and advocate who has lived through the extremes of American life—from the Polo Grounds housing projects in Harlem to the private jets of the entertainment industry's elite, from maximum-security prisons to the backstage chaos of Madison Square Garden.

Born and raised in Harlem during the crack epidemic of the 1980s, Bonds earned his nickname at fourteen and his reputation on the streets by twenty. He served time for murder as a teenager and faced federal charges in his thirties, experiencing firsthand the consequences of a life built on violence and survival. But his story didn't end there.

After his release, Bonds spent over a decade working in the music industry as head of security for Sean "Diddy" Combs, traveling the world and witnessing both the glamour   and the darkness behind the curtain of fame and fortune. He later worked with Cîroc as a brand ambassador, building the Cîroc Boys South movement and winning Ambassador of the Year after moving over one million cases across the Southern United States.

In recent years, Bonds has transformed his life experiences into a mission of service and truth-telling. He is a certified domestic violence coach, youth mentor, and motivational speaker who works directly with young people, formerly incarcerated individuals, and survivors of abuse. His approach is unflinchingly honest: he doesn't hide from his past or pretend to be perfect—instead, he uses his mistakes as teaching moments.

In 2024, Bonds was diagnosed with prostate cancer and successfully fought it into remission through a combination of conventional treatment and holistic care. This health battle, combined with his ongoing management of diabetes, reinforced his commitment to helping others before it's too late. He speaks openly about men's health, mental health, and the importance of breaking the silence around issues that too many men suffer with in private.

Bonds is the father of six children, including a newborn daughter born in 2024. He currently lives in South Carolina, where he continues his advocacy work and maintains strong connections to the Harlem community that shaped him.

Through speaking engagements, social media, and direct mentorship, Bonds reaches thousands of people who see themselves in his story—young people growing up where he grew up, men struggling with the same toxic expectations of masculinity, workers being exploited by powerful bosses, and anyone who's ever felt trapped by choices they made when they were too young to understand the consequences.

Bonds: Loyalty, Lies, and the Life That Almost Killed Me is his first book, but the story has been decades in the making. It's written for the kid who thinks jail is a rite of passage, the young woman who thinks abuse is the price of ambition, the man who's sacrificing his health and integrity for someone else's dream, and anyone who needs to know that redemption is real and it's never too late to choose yourself.

Bonds lives by a simple principle: **Word is Bond—Built on No Deception**. For him, loyalty without honesty is just complicity, and real change requires telling uncomfortable truths. He isn't perfect, and he'll tell you that himself. But he's proof that where you start doesn't determine where you finish, and that the most powerful thing you can do is tell the truth— especially when it costs you something.

Connect with Bonds: Instagram: @TheRealRogerBonds Speaking engagements and mentorship inquiries: info@1BrickPublishing.com